The Christian at Work Overseas

D1585800

The Christian at Work Overseas

A Basic Study Guide to assist in preparation

Edited by Ian Prior

11, Station Road, Teddington, Middlesex TW11 9AA Tel: 01-977 9144

The Christian at Work Overseas

Tear Fund Ltd
11 Station Road
Teddington
Middlesex TW11 9AA

© Tear Fund Ltd

First Published 1976 (Loose leaf folder)
Second Edition 1977 (Loose leaf folder)
Third Edition 1978 (Paperback)
Fourth Edition 1979 (Paperback)
Fifth Edition 1980 (Paperback)
Sixth Edition 1982 (Paperback)
ISBN 0 9506385 0 1

Printed in England by Gaffyne & Brown Ltd
Gomer Place Teddington Middlesex TW11 9AR

Contents

PART ONE: Practical

PART TWO: Theological

PART THREE: Bible Study

Appendix: Community Health

Editor's Preface

Included in this manual are selected articles by various experienced Christian workers setting out important principles of general application irrespective of your destination overseas.

You will obviously wish to gather other specific information relevant to your individual needs (e.g. the political, cultural and religious background to your country abroad). Your sponsoring society will be able to advise you further on these matters.

If this material is to be helpful then it will prove vital for you to use it as a basis for further study by informal seminar discussion groups as well as deeper personal investigation of the Scriptures. Plan to take it with you in your luggage as you leave for your assignment overseas, and in this way use it as a reference manual, as many of the issues raised in the articles will seem very remote until you are actually submerged in your new surroundings.

As you work overseas, there will be many other lessons to learn and you might wish to keep a record of these and share them with us so that future editions of this manual can be made more relevant and helpful.

My sincere thanks go to all those who have spent time from their busy schedules to contribute to this manual and to Alan Parry for his excellent illustrations.

Ian Prior

Sixth Edition - September 1982

Introduction

New countries, babbling tongues, stranger customs, and all reached with magic carpet swiftness, are exciting in prospect and easily retain their novelty for the passing tourist who retails his experiences with a mixture of pride, awe, humour and exaggeration.

Whatever there may have been of romance in the initial motivation of the short or long term Christian worker overseas, he quickly learns that the novelty is not permanent. He has got to face realistically and determinedly the task of living for Christ in a different culture and climate when his normally successful verbal armoury is completely ineffective.

It is to help such workers to prepare for what is involved spiritually and physically, intellectually and culturally, politically and socially, that this handbook has been prepared. The briefest glance at its contents is sufficient to show that there is much more to going overseas to witness for Christ than an air ticket and a nicely packed suitcase. Every article in the handbook is valuable, to be read in preparation and to be re-read again and again as each new situation or problem has to be faced. The writers are men and women whose experience can be relied upon.

While the long term worker will have longer in which to learn all that is needed to make a success of the job, the short term worker also needs to be successful and cannot hide behind such thoughts as "I'm only here for a year or two so it doesn't really matter if I don't learn the language — they seem to understand my signs and grimaces!"

Christian service demands the highest degree of preparation and preparedness.

Ernest Oliver

General Secretary of The Evangelical Missionary Alliance
Associate Director — Tear Fund

9

A More Excellent Way

Edgar Stoesz in 'Beyond Good Intentions' (with gratitude to St. Paul)

We may speak the language of sacrifice and of service, but if we have no love in our hearts for those whom we seek to help, our efforts will have no more effect than a noisy gong or a clanging cymbal whose influence fades away with its clamour.

We may emphasise the urgency of development, comprehend all the urgent problems and needs of the world, and have such absolute faith and determination that we can imagine the masses living in prosperous communities at a respectable standard of living, but if we have no love for the people, it is all in vain.

We may distribute all the aid we possess. We may give our lives to save the needy masses, but if love is not our motive, the world will be none the better for our effort.

With love we will be very patient as we confront a foreign culture with change.

With love we will not feel boastfully righteous as though we have all the solutions to the world's needs.

With love we will never assert our superiority, never selfishly seek praise for sharing with others that with which we have been so abundantly blessed.

With love we will never inflate our ego at the expense of those we have come to serve.

With love we will always be slow to expose the failures and weaknesses of others.

With love we will not be resentful when our service is taken for granted.

With love our efforts will hit the mark.

Love never gives up. As for teaching, it will be superseded; as for agencies of development, they will cease. For our technology and our planning and our institutions are incomplete but when our actions are guided by love and justice, then they will be complete.

We are limited in our understanding, we see in a mirror dimly. We are baffled by problems and lasting solutions elude us. But we are learning bit by bit and we long for the day when love shall rule the world.

Thus faith that God has a plan for the world, hope that seeks the full life for all, and love that knows no boundaries – these three endure – but the greatest of these is love. Make love your goal.

The value of service is not measured by the time, but by the quality of obedience it represents, the standard of love and identification and the extent of sharing of the life of Christ

PART ONE:

Practical

Self·Analysis

Your Motives

What are your aims in going overseas?

1　Escapism; independence; adventure; to see the world; mountaineering(!).
2　Involvement with a different culture on an equal footing.
3　To find out what others think of my native land.
4　To improve race relations.
5　Vague Do Goodism.
6　To help a developing country (the volunteer's imperative!).
7　To evangelise.

8　To serve Christ in a new environment.
9　To see if my Christian faith is relevant to the needs of others.
10　To see if my Christian faith is relevant to *my* need in their circumstances.
11　To learn from God in witnessing in strange circumstances.
12　To understand the problems of Christian churches overseas.
13　To see missionaries in action.
14　To find out my future sphere of service.

Your Attitudes

From: 'You can so get there from here' (MARC)

How do you react?

1 If I were a "foreign missionary", would I be able to train citizen Christians to take over *all* my work and then leave them alone and go somewhere else?

2 Does what the Lord is doing through me actually reach to people around the world in some *practical, beneficial* way *now*?

3 Do I regard other people and different ways of their doing things as an opportunity for personal growth no matter how intensely they may repulse me during my initial reaction?

4 What three things can I do *right away* to make the goals for my world of contacts the same as Christ's goals for His world?

5 Am I preparing myself to really contribute anything fresh and creative to meeting the needs of fellow human beings through new and unexpected opportunities overseas or am I willing to accept the status quo?

6 Does God really care about whether or not I care about every person in the world?

7 Are my personal goals more important to me than seeing the needs of human beings recognised and fulfilled?

8 Does my personal God care enough about what has not yet happened to begin to prepare me *now* for helping to meet future, unexpected needs?

9 Am I as interested in the total well-being of whole human beings as I am in winning them to my specific faith or way of thinking?

10 Am I so threatened or intimidated by the complex and by the unknown that I cannot constructively reach out to other human beings in their needs?

11 Is world need as consciously real to me as local need?

12 Do I regularly find it impossible to care now about persons whose needs, fears and pains are outside my firsthand experience?

13 Do I make a point of knowing what's going on in the world so I can care that more than 3.6 billion individual human beings are affected by the forces involved?

14 Do I regard changes in the way of life around me as automatically suspect or do I see them as new doors of opportunity to relate to people and their needs?

15 Do I care enough about the seriousness of eternal human conservation to step back regularly and question what I am doing and how Christ can improve it?

Your First Impressions

Taken from 'Expatriates Abroad' by M E Gass
First produced by the UCCF Overseas Information Service, but now out of print

The Hero (or Heroine)

Romantic halo; admiring relatives and friends; uplifting church commissioning . . .

The Nobody who knows he is

N.B. None of these may hit you. All won't. Some may.

1 Fear of 'plane; dread of first day.
2 Heat and humidity.
3 Unwelcome and unwelcomed? Resented and resisted?
4 Loneliness.
5 Sickness, headache, dysentery, bites.
6 Hard work, poor accommodation, foreign food, dreary scenery, money stolen (all one man's experience!)
7 Initial failure to communicate.
Inability to adjust may lead to cynicism or despair and even loss of faith.

The Nobody who thinks he's somebody

1 Over-enthusiastic and under-imaginative.
2 Irritatingly cheerful.
3 Back-slapping hearty bonhomie.
4 Knows all the answers.
5 Dispenses advice regardless.
6 Drapes arm paternally over shoulders of older and more experienced nationals.
7 Treads on everybody's toes.

Humpty Dumpty had a great fall!

A missionary wrote recently to a young couple newly going abroad "Be prepared for everything to be totally different from what you expected". This is true for anyone going to a developing country. It has been called 'culture shock'.

The Christian at Work Overseas

You may be pleasantly surprised

1 You may find yourself in a highly sophisticated society – which may sap your spiritual vitality!

2 You may find that even the most simple people have high standards of *essential* social behaviour – backward perhaps in hygiene but well ahead in good manners, respect for older people, kindness to children, strong family feeling, good neighbourliness, tribal discipline, courage and endurance.

3 You will certainly find high standards of morality practised by many who take their non-Christian religions seriously – from whatever motive, e.g. almsgiving – a means of merit with Muslims; respect for 'life' – among Hindus; abounding hospitality and just plain honest-to-goodness kindness.

4 You will often find that the educated rising generation in all developing countries has ideas, ideals and interests much like your own.

5 You will be amazed at the self-sacrifice of parents who want their children to have a good education.

You may be genuinely shocked

1 At sudden reversions to violent outbursts, superstitions (witchcraft), even demonology and sometimes violent manifestations of hate where moments before all had been calm.

2 At widespread immorality among the young due to:
a the sudden impact of Western education and freedom and the consequent breakdown of family discipline;
b irresponsibility caused by earlier slavery and temptation brought by the predatory expatriate male.
Watch your own standards; they can easily slip.

3 At unpunctuality – especially with transport and meals – and unreliability – especially in the use of your possessions (e.g. a borrowed bicycle may be used by the whole family and friends as well), and in the paying of debts. Usually, don't lend what you are not prepared to give.

4 At the position of women:
a sometimes excluded from social gatherings in the home.
b still the burden-bearer in most of Africa.
c wives are still being beaten there too.

5 At nepotism ('brotherisation'), tribalism, bribery and lack of experience and even of integrity in important positions.

6 At self-conscious, even pugnacious nationalism, and a tendency to touchiness because of this.

7 At their sense of humour – they may laugh if you fall down, even if you hurt yourself, but they will also help you up. Some people laugh when actually they are embarrassed.

Self-Analysis

So what do you do?

1 Quickly shed preconceived ideas, especially about European superiority: learn to look at Western civilization both objectively and through the eyes of non-Europeans.

2 Avoid slick judgments: you won't learn much that's really basic in one year, or even two.

3 Avoid either extreme withdrawal or extreme identification: the first will be regarded as pride, the second as foolishness.

4 Don't show your shock!

5 Show strict integrity in your own conduct: behind polite acceptance of the white stranger there will be the cool eye of assessment, and if you offend, strong feelings of outrage.

6 Use your eyes and your imagination: teaching sixth formers in sandals and shorts may seem sensible to you in hot weather but it may earn your headmaster's disapproval; a mini-skirt and flowing locks may be accepted – or rather tolerated – in a large town but they could cause a riot in an up-country school. Even eating with both hands can be non-U in parts of India!

7 Be careful in the use of language: non-Europeans are on the whole more scrupulous about politeness than are Westerners, e.g. words like idiot, monkey, silly, fool, black (to describe evil), white (to describe something good) can give great offence, even in the classroom.

8 Try not to get involved in politics. Be careful about criticising or comparing social and political conditions, especially at the local levels. One of those responsible may be a relation of one of your listeners! Mind what you write in your letters; in some countries they may be opened and you may lose your job; or what you write may be repeated in Britain in the hearing of an overseas student from your area – the world is a smaller place than ever these days.

9 Beware of joining a European clique of moaners and critics.

10 Don't get into the habit of complaining about a certain person or situation: it may become an obsession. Pray about it or him.

11 Don't be biassed either pro- or anti-European. There is such a thing as gratitude. Both you and the people you are helping owe much to the European.

12 And remember that although Western culture should not be confused with Christianity, the *best* of the West is probably the result of Christianity.

13 God's standards don't change, but you will need some resilience in interpreting them in a different environment.

14 Your great advantage over the non-Christian is that all things work together for good for those who love God.

You are like this

Notes from a talk by Bishop Misaeri Kauma, Uganda

The expatriate as seen through the eyes of nationals

1 The national's viewpoint may be conditioned by his background: historical, (especially his previous experience of expatriate government officials, farmers and missionaries), political (that of a young, self-conscious nation), moral, religious and economic. The expatriate should therefore learn what he can about these and modify his opinions and actions accordingly.

2 The old expatriate father-figure and Jack-of-all-trades has been replaced by the expert in a limited field whose help is only needed sometimes, and who must learn to act as a fellow-worker or subordinate.

3 He may be suspected at first of neo-colonialism. The church leader may also be a political leader. He may remember when missionaries were regarded by nationalists as being identified with colonialists and he may suspect that you are going to rob him of his new-found freedom – if not politically, then personally.

4 There are two types of church leaders: the older, usually uneducated, wanting advice and help, though not ready for new ideas, and the new young ones, enlightened, independent, resentful of interference or domination, but ready for ideas if suggested tactfully and humbly.

5 Be careful not to force a policy, especially if you represent an organisation giving money. All gifts must be without strings – as to the Lord.

6 The ordinary villagers will be very friendly and ready to talk.

7 Brotherhood in Christ is the best way of acceptance – learning from each other.

8 There is no culture in the world that is Christian, but it is Christ who transforms any culture into His own.

9 You can be a mediator between different races, tribes and denominations.

10 You are expected to act as a responsible representative of a long-established church and a country with an ancient Christian tradition.

11 Try to conquer your British reserve, which can be mistaken for pride or independence, or superiority. Overcome any barrier by asking people to pray for you in a difficulty.

12 Be a loving link in the chain of the kingdom of God.

What will you learn?

These are some of the lessons learnt by those who contributed to the book 'We all volunteered' published by the Scripture Union in 1967.

What others have learned

1 Inadequate values, though held for a life-time, transformed in a matter of moments.
2 Independence, housekeeping, budgeting, organisation of time and leisure.
3 Discipline and tact in small everyday affairs.
4 Appreciation of home comforts previously taken for granted

5 Responsibility for others.
6 Self-knowledge, leading to more maturity.
7 Humility and thankfulness after watching a fingerless and toeless leprosy patient praising and thanking God.
8 Understanding the importance of perceiving the essential man, stripped of his cultural trappings.
9 Realisation that the people and the small everyday things are the real Africa.
10 Tolerance of other races' elaborate politeness, leisureliness and demanding laws of hospitality.
11 Respect for a different culture and the best in their religion.
12 Respect for even the most primitive social system.
13 The importance of not condemning any other way of life before it is fully understood.
14 The need to divorce Christianity from Western culture.
15 The necessity of earning the right to speak.

16 Sympathy for the lonely foreigner in Britain.
17 More thought about the problems in other parts of the world.
18 Appreciation of the wonders of God's creation.
19 Utter dependence on Christ.

First Impressions & Culture Shock

Adjustment in other Cultures

by The Rev Canon Alan Neech

Going to live in another culture can be a traumatic experience. These notes are intended to point out the sort of problems that will be encountered and the usual reactions to them.

For the short term worker problems are not usually intense. Like all visitors and early arrivals they are fascinated by everything they see. There are others at hand who can guide and communicate. When things are difficult for any reason, the thought that this will not last longer than a few months or a year or two at most, helps to make things tolerable. Nevertheless what follows does apply to some extent even to short-termers. Incidentally, short term workers should always be sensitive to the possibility of long term workers with whom they serve being tempted to harbour thoughts of resentment or even jealousy. "It's all very well for them. They will be off in a few months but I have to stick this out for years."

Physical conditions must neither be under-rated or over-rated. Learning how to live in a *very hot climate* takes longer than you'd think. You may surprise yourself at the way you can get irritated and angry when the temperature stays high. *Changes in altitude* too can have strange effects. Water boils at lower temperatures at high altitudes. and baking requires new understanding. You will be breathless at first and may feel very lethargic. But beware of blaming all your failures on the altitude or the heat!

You will almost certainly be *lonely* at times. This may be because of language or other barriers. *You* must make special efforts to relate to others, even fellow missionaries across a yawning generation gap.

It may be that you will not have *a clearly defined role* in spite of the job description you insisted on before you left home. What is really expected of you and of your wife by your colleagues and by the local church?

The emotional disturbance which often comes in the early days of adjustment to a different culture is called *culture shock*. It comes because we just do not know how to take our place in the new society and how to behave in our new surroundings. Every culture has many subtle signs by which we know our place and how we should react to those around us. Now, just like a child, you have everything to learn — how to walk, sit, greet people, receive visitors, accept or refuse gifts and invitations and many other things.

Language problems lie at the heart of much culture shock. Not understanding what is being said you wonder whether they are talking about you. They probably are! Some Eastern languages are difficult enough to learn but you often have also to learn where your listener comes in the social scale to know how to address him correctly. You are reduced to the level of a child again. After months of language study you still cannot have an intelligent conversation. You cannot do much more than talk about the price of a pound of rice. And this after the responsible job you had at home. There is often a temptation to reject a language during these early months. It becomes easy to blame language teachers and methods to excuse personal failures here.

There are three recognisable stages through which people go as they settle in to life in another culture.

Fascination

Everything is different — sights, smells and sounds. Short term residents and visitors do not get beyond this stage.

Hostility

Hostility emerges when the initial fascination wears off and when we are no longer surrounded by others to protect and guide us. Then tensions build up. Everyday minor irritations become symbols of the inferiority and inefficiency of the new land. A poor water supply, irregular transport, unreliable electricity supply and other such things become subjects for constant complaint and fault-finding.

This is the time when homesickness begins to be felt. The host country is so bad. At home everything is wonderful! Homesickness has strange manifestations. A longing for English food not available locally (cornflakes for instance) and little symbols of home (a little Union Jack over the mantelpiece) can well be expressions of homesickness.

People sometimes become obsessed with cleanliness.

Hostility of the kind we are considering expresses itself in *rebellion against authority*, whether of local church leaders, colleagues in the work or committees at home. Real or imagined grievances are nursed. Remorseless criticism of everything and everybody is the ingredient of daily conversation. When there is personal failure, it is all somebody else's fault.

In extreme cases there can be such a sense of failure, compounded by guilt because of the criticisms made of others, that the sufferer from culture shock wants to give up altogether. He blames himself and becomes thoroughly introverted and is sure that his feeling depressed is spiritual failure. What a relief it is to be reminded that depression can be due to homesickness, or to separation from family and loved ones, or even follow some of the infections you may likely get.

What a blessing a sense of humour is! When you can laugh at a problem it begins to look different. Tensions within lessen and healing processes begin.

Bi-culturalism

Bi-culturalism is the time when with at least some of the local language learned and enough understanding of the new society absorbed to know how to live, you can begin to feel "at home" in your new environment. This can take years of course. Many of your previously accepted standards will need revising. Different cultures have different expectations of the new missionary. When he was asked what quality he looked for first in a new arrival, a Nigerian said that the one quality most desired was respect for elders. A man could have love, adaptability, sensitivity, a Spirit-filled life, but if he failed to show respect no one would listen to him.

Early months and years in a new environment are often a chance to discover oneself and this can well be a shock in itself. For some there has to come a frank facing of defeat. If this is accompanied by a recommitment to Christ, who takes us as we are and moulds us to become the persons He can use, the unhappinesses of culture shock will not have been in vain. Rather they will have been an important part of God's refining processes and you can come through immeasurably enriched.

It's Not All a Picnic!

by The Rev Eric Wright
Whilst acting as an itinerant pastor to workers in Ethiopia

This article is written out of eight months of travelling around Ethiopia, visiting community development programmes, viewing situations and listening to the tales that the short term workers had to tell. The article highlights various pressures that have seemed to be the common lot of these workers. It does not seek to provide answers or even hints as to how people should prepare themselves to meet the problems. These problems can't be prepared for in the last few weeks before departure! They demand years of simply getting to know the Lord in a progressively deeper way. He whose life has been characterised by that growing intimacy will have nothing to fear! However, the article, uncovering some of the tensions that the short term worker will have to cope with, is written in the conviction that to be fore-warned is to be fore-armed. To be taken by surprise and to discover the reality of the pressures, after having glibly assumed that the difficulties would be rendered negligible by the size of the thrilling new experiences awaiting one, can in itself knock one completely off balance. On the other hand, to anticipate the areas of tension and warfare can mean that they are met with a calm poise which will put one into an advantageous position for the battle.

The dreaded array of last minute goodbyes has been safely negotiated. The anticipated pain of final parting was less acute than might have been expected, as the barrier into the departure lounge was passed. The short term worker begins to relax a little in the padded Boeing seat, excited by this materialising of dreams, as the jet whisks its human cargo away from the homeland across Europe and into a continent beyond. On this day the sights have been set for so long! So many preparations have at last been completed in spite of the once seeming impossibility of getting all the last minute things done "in just three more days". Yes, the adventure of serving the Lord for two years in a completely new environment, in a foreign land, has begun. Thoughts, hopes, fears and prayers mingle in the mind as the journey progresses. Amongst other matters there crops up from time to time the question of what sorts of new pressures and battles will have to be faced.

Committing oneself to short term missionary work is not to be regarded as equivalent to embracing a life of total deprivation for two years! Far from it! Not a few times one will undoubtedly chuckle inwardly at the "sacrifices of missionary life", as one enjoys to the full some experience or some luxury which one could never have at home.

And yet there will be deprivations to be coped with. And there will be times when the lack of mod-cons will become a source of aggravation. A seatless toilet – or should I say a hole in the ground?! – is all right some days: but it is not some days: it is every day! Or it can be an invigorating experience to live the simple life for a while and to have to collect every drop of water that you use from the nearby stream. But it soon becomes a bind, carrying those heavy buckets; and some days the water is horribly muddy if the cattle have got there first: and it's a chore boiling all the drinking water for twenty minutes: and then it all has to be strained through dishcloths: clean dishcloths every day! How one longs after a while for a sink, a tap and clear running water! Or it looks so luxurious – and undoubtedly it is – when the truck unloads half a dozen crates of tinned food in the camp. But what would one not give for some fresh fruit and vegetables and for some reprieve from the goat meat which is the only fresh food to be found in many miles?! Little things which can easily be coped with occasionally, especially when one is feeling good, can become big obstacles when they are part and parcel of an inescapable daily routine and when one is weary and washed out. Don't think that, because you've always been the camping holiday, "good-to-rough-it" type of person that you'll be exempt! The mere business of living in these "simple" conditions will be a threat to your peace and joy at some time or another. The Devil will attempt to discourage you thereby. But praise God! – He plans to teach you, as you run to Him, the grace that enables one truly to say "I have learned in whatever state I am, therewith to be content".

Allied to living conditions is health. The new arrival in tropical climes can scarcely hope to escape at least some minor upsets in his digestive system! It is, strangely, almost easier to cope with a week, flat on one's back with 'flu' after which one bounces back to normal health, than it is to cope with the diarrhoeas and amoebas which hardly send one to bed, but which drain one of emotional and physical energy. There's something about being far from home and family that makes illness more difficult to accept. And then there is the heat. In some places this is a real energy-draining factor that quite simply leaves one unable to do the same amount of work that one happily did at home. It can be hard coming to terms with new restrictions that climatic conditions lay upon one. The conscientious may find it particularly hard to accept a reduction in the level of work output. To have learned at home to truly live with oneself and to accept oneself, with one's limitations as well as one's strengths, just as Christ Himself has accepted us as we are, will prove an enormous benefit in making these necessary adjustments. He who can not really relax with an easy conscience, make full use of his rest hours, absorb himself in outside interests and hobbies for a while, may have to learn to do so for maximum efficiency of service.

Then there is the area of loneliness. He would be the exception rather than the rule who did not find that here was a front on which he had to fight new battles and assert new victories. There will often be enough of excitement and adventure in the first few weeks of one's new assignment to take some of the sting out of the parting from family and close friends. But when one begins to settle down, often in an isolated, remote place, probably with only a handful of others with whom you can communicate in your mother tongue, the picture can be very different. One cannot choose one's friends under such circumstances. You just have to get on well with your fellow workers. Yearnings may

well arise for the depth and quality of the friendships one has left behind. One may find oneself longing for the companionship of someone to whom one could really tell one's frustrations and feelings. Perhaps the desire to be married will assume proportions unimagined before – how desirable to have somebody really close to one! And yet the choice of marriage partners has suddenly diminished before your eyes to nothingness! Yes, there will more than likely be new areas of loneliness to learn to live with. But here also, as this problem sends you running into Jesus' arms, is a wonderful new opportunity of finding in Him a quality of friendship and companionship that otherwise you might never have sought.

This loneliness will have its spiritual aspect as well, in the form of a sudden lack of pastoral encouragement from older Christians, and in the lack of regular ministry and Bible teaching. Church services, now unattainable, will seem a more precious means of grace to you than ever they seemed before. Now you will recognise in a new light the value of having the Bible expounded and explained, and your own ability to dig into the Word and to feed yourself will be stretched and tested. Yet another field appears of course, in which to learn how much God Himself, being no man's debtor, is well able to open up to you, in your isolated circumstances, His Word by His Spirit, but the discovery may well be accompanied by heartache and tears.

Many pressures can be accepted in the assurance that one is doing a useful job. If one can be sure that one's service is vitally needed and is making a really valid contributior to people's needs and to God's work, one can happily cope with many difficulties. But it often doesn't seem this way at first. It takes time to get into a new job. The first weeks may involve a lot of ground-work in carving out a niche that really fits your capabilities. You may well have pressed upon you more responsibility than you expected, or on the other hand you may be made so subject to authority that you feel stifled and unable to stretch yourself. There will be a good deal of adjusting to do on your part and on the part of the mission for which you are working, and this will demand a fair amount of patience, especially in the early days when job satisfaction could be so important to your overall disposition. One naturally feels that the short term nature of one's commitment accentuates the need to become quickly proficient in one's work, and the exercise of the necessary patience may not come altogether easily!

The language barrier will also add a dimension of frustration to the work. Have you not come to serve these people? And here you are dependent on an interpreter for any meaningful communication. Even if you have a period of language study you will hardly be a fluent conversationalist within your two-year appointment! Yes, if one was convinced of the quality of the job one was doing, and if one could truly communicate with the people, some of the hard living conditions would become more tolerable. But here is the challenge: when my contribution seems such a drop in the ocean, and when I can hardly say more than "good morning" in my Yorkshire accent, can I learn to draw on the appropriate resources of God that will keep me rejoicing in Him?

So many pressures and tensions to be faced! But don't run away! See them for what they most certainly can be — God-given opportunities to enlarge one's faith and to find in Him as one has never found before a perfect sufficiency. For "His strength is made perfect in weakness", and "we have this treasure in earthen vessels, that the transcendent power may be seen to belong to God and not to us". Is that not, after all, the aim of all our service? — that men may see Him. And this is His divinely appointed means! What capital these pressures and difficulties are — in the powerful hands of God.

Dear Mum...

First impressions of life in Imaginabad

The following are quotations from letters written home from the capital city of a developing nation during the first few months of a Christian's short term assignment there in connection with a Christian Relief Organisation.

1

P.O. Box 787,
Imaginabad.

6th March.

Dear Mum,

... and oh, yes! I promised that I would let you know whether I experienced any of what they call culture shock! Well, personally, I think it is all a bit of a myth! Of course there *are* hordes of really poor people here and they tell me that once you get off the main streets it's pretty squalid, but I was prepared for all that. It's sad to see so many people begging, but once again I did know that this was how it would be. I think that to be prepared beforehand is really the answer. I mean, I *do* care about all the poverty and the hard lives that people have – but it doesn't disturb me or throw me off balance the way that people warned me it would.

I don't know whether putting up with the weather falls into the realm of culture shock or not – some people seem to think it does. There again it *is* hot and steamy and sticky but I didn't expect it to be any different and I don't find it too hard to bear.

I'm pleasantly surprised to find that a lot of people speak English and imagine that I won't need to bother too much about learning the language, which is a bit of a relief – all the educated people have done some of their schooling in English.

So don't worry about me, Mum – I'm not dying of culture shock! That will have to be all for now.

All my love and prayers,

from MIKE

2

P.O. Box 787,
Imaginabad.

19th March.

Dear Mum,

... You're right! (I can just hear you saying 'Aren't I always?'!!) It's not all as painless being here as I thought it was going to be! There *are* quite a few things that really upset me, if I'm honest.

I told you about the house we live in. I was surprised at first that we should live in such a plush house — so utterly different from all that we had been told about squalor and poverty! But deep down I was quite relieved that our living conditions were so good. Only now that I've been around a bit more and seen for myself how little other people in this country have, I don't know how I can reconcile myself to having so much space and luxury. They say that the administrative committee has been over this ground repeatedly and still think that this is the most suitable kind of housing, all things considered. But I feel that one can too easily learn to accept this and I don't think I want to! I'm sure you feel things particularly strongly to begin with, and I was so annoyed yesterday when someone told me I should hold my tongue till I've been here for six months. Surely newcomers like me can see things that the old stagers become blind to.

As I said last time, I'd been warned about the poverty here. But it's *our luxury* that bothers me! Nobody ever told me that I'd be living in a house with two full-time and two part-time servants. I can see the benefit of giving people work in this society, but you wouldn't believe how little we pay them. I'm told that we can only pay them at the rate which nationals would give, but I can't for the life of me see why we don't set a good example and pay more.

I suppose that you can see from this that I'm a bit at loggerheads with some of the other foreigners here. In fact I find it easier to get on well with the nationals. The sad thing is that it's not only in my case that tensions exist. So many of the foreigners don't seem to get on well with each other. Maybe THIS is culture shock! I hadn't expected this. I mean, we all got on so well together in the Youth Fellowship at home. I *do* miss St. Jude's — there's nothing here like the mutual love and fellowship that you have in the church at home. I did know that missionaries were ordinary people with their fair share of personality problems etc., but I expected them at least to get on well with each other and to have a real love for the people here. I am quite sure that more prayer is made for Imaginabad at St. Jude's than is made here. I don't mean to paint a black picture of my colleagues, Mum — they're a great bunch and I get on well with them on the whole. Did I tell you that Tom, the pharmacist here used to go out with Sandra's friend, Nancy? ...

Look after yourself. I miss you too,

Love from MIKE

3

P.O. Box 787,
Imaginabad.

2nd April.

Dear Mum,

... Now, to answer some of your questions! I'm sorry if I don't always answer all of your question marks! Yes, of course I read your letters – avidly!! No, there's no difference between Moslem and Muslim. Yes, we do eat a lot of rice, but you can also get bread. Tom's surname is Bonthram-Burroughs, believe it or not! Oh, and no, most of the people here have not been to Bible College.

Mind you on that last question, I'm not at all sure that that would make any difference. I think we know a lot of theory – it's just working out our Christian convictions in practice in a situation like this that is so difficult. It strikes me that one of the problems is this – that to want to come and work in a place like this you have to be pretty individualistic and go-ahead. Now when you throw a lot of people like that together there are bound to be clashes of personality. Our organisation can't run smoothly without a reasonable authority structure, and I notice that the sort of people who come on this sort of assignment like to run their own show. Sometimes I'm sure that grows out of an uncertainty about what they're meant to be doing, and out of having a lot more responsibility than they've ever had before. Look at me with seventeen nationals working under me, at the tender age of twenty-six! Mum, I really pray that I'll act towards those in authority over me as I expect these nationals to act towards me. I sometimes feel that the whole project here is a bit of a circus with every man doing what is right in his own eyes! It's funny, back at Wolfe and Willcox one didn't expect so much, but having come to work in a Christian organisation, one expects it to be so different – and indeed it needs to be different if we are to cut any spiritual ice in this hard situation.

Thanks again for the food parcel, but really there are very few things that are unavailable here.

Love to all the others as well as to yourself,

from MIKE

4

P.O. Box 787,
Imaginabad.

30th April.

Dear Mum,

I'm sorry for being so long in writing! The truth is that I've had a bout of amoebic dysentry! Yes, already!! But don't worry – that just puts me into the category of 'normal'! Most people don't last two months without being afflicted. The cure – a dreaded pill called Flagyll – was considerably worse than the disease by my way of thinking, but I'm back to normal again – fighting fit and ready for some more hard work. I must admit I was pretty depressed last week. The doctor told me that this was a side effect of Flagyll, but I suppose it was another side effect of Flagyll that I refused to believe him and insisted that I was suffering from culture shock. Well, maybe one's first attack of amoeba *is* culture shock!! ...

... Actually, to get back to the culture shock discussion, Mum, this month has been far more difficult than the first one was. I guess things affect different people in different ways. I remember saying to you that I'd come prepared for poverty, beggars, squalor, tropical heat etc., and so they hadn't affected me. Let me tell you about yesterday. Yesterday was *really* hot. I got up at 7.00 and was dripping with heat in no time at all. I started the day with a shower (the first of three) but it's impossible to get properly dry. Actually I remember it was like this the first week I arrived, but standing it for one week is a different proposition to standing it day in day out for months on end. To get back to yesterday, though, I spent part of the day at the clinic where Fiona and Ruth work. It was really upsetting to see so many malnourished children, and I felt so acutely yesterday that anything we do is such a drop in the ocean. By the time I got home from my own work I was absolutely exhausted and drained of energy. I know I should have taken a rest at lunch time but I wanted to finish mending a bike and I never feel up to anything but bed after supper these days, and lunch time is the only time for doing personal tasks. Well, anyway when I came home last night, I sat down on my bed and for no apparent reason I just began to cry like a child – something I can't ever remember happening before. It felt so silly, but somehow it helped! I can't quite put my finger on what was wrong – I'm sure it was a combination of being physically drained by the weather and emotionally drained by the awful human suffering we see around us every day. To be honest I think that the last straw that broke this camel's back was that I'd asked the cook to make steamed pudding for our supper and he dished up caramel custard which as you know, I can't stand! I get so frustrated these days with my inability to communicate, and I'm still finding language study a painful slog!

Well, Mum, maybe I'll not be so quick in future to dismiss culture shock as being non-existant. Mind you, I still think it is a silly term!

Love as always,

from MIKE

Personal Health & Hygiene

Notes on Health

by Miss Anne Cooper

It is important to realise that health is one of our most effective weapons, and will therefore be subject to attack. This is particularly true in a foreign environment to which one's body needs to adapt. It is also particularly true when one goes from a comparatively 'hot-house' environment into the hazards of a developing country. Some illnesses cannot be prevented, but others can. It is a Christian responsibility to guard the health of ourselves and, in some cases, of other people too, not with morbid introspection, but with watchfulness and common sense.

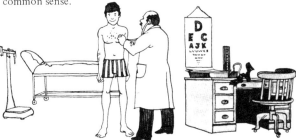

Here are some of the basic rules:

As in other spheres, preparation is important. Almost all organisations sending people overseas require a pre-departure medical check. This should also include a dental check. If one has, or suspects, any medical problems this is the time to bring them into the open, and to obtain expert advice.

(p.63ff)   This is also the time for the immunisation routine. It should be started 6—8 weeks before departure. The exact routine depends on the area in which one will be serving. It always includes smallpox, cholera and typhoid immunisation. For the latter two, two injections at 10—14 days interval are needed. They are usually combined in this country.

33

Smallpox vaccination can be given at the time of the first injection. Immuno-globulin is now generally accepted to be a wise precaution against infective hepatitis (jaundice). It should not be given until 4—6 weeks after the other immunisation, hence the need to start early.

Other types of immunisation which may be required, and about which you should ask your doctor, are: yellow fever; tetanus toxide; polio, BCG.

Your own society will give you detailed guidance concerning your immunisation programme.

Certain diseases and conditions are more common in other parts of the world than in our own countries. This means that we have little resistance to them and need to take precautions, especially when we first arrive and take up our assignments.

Intestinal Problems

(p.19ff) There are a number of infections and parasites which can be ingested, and which cause varying degrees of discomfort. The important things to know are how to avoid these tummy upsets, and when they are serious and require specific treatment and medical advice. Occasional, comparatively mild, upsets are almost inevitable. Any attack, however, which is accompanied by severe vomiting, or does not clear up within 48 hours, or recurs within one month, necessitates medical treatment.

It is also a good thing to check one's weight. Any undue, or continuous loss of weight needs reporting.

(p.26ff) Intestinal problems are due to infection being taken in with food and drink. Water and milk *must* be boiled before use, then kept in a covered container. It is as well to obtain a bottle of water-sterilising tablets which can be used on journeys, but not as a regular means of sterilising. It is necessary to allow 20—30 minutes for the tablets to purify the water.

Tea is a great standby, and is comparatively free from infection, particularly in countries where the milk and sugar are boiled in it. Bottled drinks such as Coca-Cola and Fanta are also usually safe. One should, however, avoid local brands.

Special care must be taken over the preparation of food. Raw foods, such as salads and certain types of fruit are difficult to clean and should be avoided. It is a good rule to eat food which has been seen cooking and is eaten still hot. Occasionally it is necessary, in order to keep the rules of hospitality, to eat unwisely. If so, a prophylactic dose of a drug such as Entero-Vioform should be taken. One usually finds, however, that others understand the weakness of the volunteer's stomach and make allowances for this.

Fever

(p.32ff) Unexplained fever occurs fairly frequently. Unless it is prolonged it is usually sufficient to retire to bed with a couple of aspirins. In some areas there is still a risk of malaria. If

working in one of these, anti-malarial drugs should be taken, and advice will be given concerning this.

The screening of doors and windows with netting, and the use of mosquito nets is also essential in some areas.

Fatigue

(p.16ff) It is usual to experience a certain amount of fatigue while adjusting to a new climate and environment. Sleeplessness may be a problem brought about by heat, noise or insects. Another obvious cause of tiredness is over-work. It is important to have a rest day each week, and to take normal holidays. A change of scenery often does wonders. It will be good too to get around and see something of the country as a whole.

Just as there are physical strains there are also mental and emotional ones, and we need to be just as watchful about them as about physical ills. Prolonged sleeplessness is one of the danger signs. Others are exceptional anxiety or undue depression. If such symptoms are present a person would benefit from help. Not necessarily psychiatric treatment, but talking things over with a mature Christian friend.

Heat

(p.10ff) Some countries have much hotter climates than we are used to, in which case one feels as if one is getting into the oven in place of the Sunday joint when one steps outside or lands from a plane. Care must be taken to protect oneself by always standing in the shade when possible, by covering one's head with a light scarf when in direct sunlight, and by wearing dark glasses. It is also important to keep up the fluid intake and particularly to take extra salt. A teaspoonful, or a salt tablet can be put in a glass of water and will not, under these circumstances, taste unpleasant.

If headaches occur it is wise to stay inside in the comparative cool, and to take a dose of aspirin.

Prickly heat is another problem, particularly when the climate is humid. Frequent washing is important, and prickly-heat powder should be used.

Recommended simple medical kit to carry with you

Aspirin or Paracetamol — for pain and fevers
Anti-malarial
Elastoplast dressing strip
Crepe bandage for sprains or emergency sling
Antiseptic cream (Acriflex) for infected wounds or bites or burns
Anti-histamine tablets for allergies
Insect repellent cream
Salt tablets
Kaolin and Streptomycin mixture for simple diarrhoea
Multi-vitamins can be taken daily if diet is not very adequate
Strepsils or other antiseptic lozenges for sore throats
Marzine or Kwells for travel sickness
Sterotabs (Boots) for emergency water purification

The above notes are just a brief summary. You are also advised to read the book "Preservation of personal health in warm climates" - the relevant page numbers are put in these notes. The book may be obtained from:
The Ross Institute of Tropical Medicine
London School of Hygiene and Tropical Medicine
Keppel Street (Gower Street)
London WC1E 7HT

Dealing with Depression

Written by Dr Ken Moynagh for Crusade Magazine
(also in 'Man of two worlds – the life of Ken Moynagh' published by Walters)

Depression is not a disease but a symptom. The illness that causes it may be mainly physical, like glandular fever, or mainly psychological, as in many mental illnesses, or spiritual, as when John Bunyan's Christian fell into the Slough of Despond. Commonly all these threads contribute to the tangle that has to be unravelled, and to overlook any one of them hinders recovery.

Christians often think that to be depressed means that something must be wrong spiritually. Because of this attitude the sufferer finds that at a time when he most feels the need of love and understanding he is surrounded by Job's comforters whose well-meaning efforts only deepen the wounds they are trying to heal. His sense of isolation is aggravated because God seems unreal. Prayer, worship and the Bible become empty and irrelevant, and his faith flickers like a candle in the wind. The past mocks him, the future frightens him and the present imprisons him in the gloom of despair.

Anxiety and Depression

Doctors distinguish between depression caused by mental illness (psychotic depression) and depression in a healthy person caused by stress (reactive or neurotic depression).[1] 'It is called reactive because it represents a reaction to some external event, such as the loss of a relative; it is neurotic because it is much stronger and longer-lasting than would be appropriate. Depression represents an emotional over-reaction: anxiety is forward looking and concerned with fears for the future; depression is backward looking and concerned with sadness about the past — the two states are usually found together in the same person'.

In this article we will not be dealing with mental illness (psychotic depression) but with the much commoner reactive depression.

Although the whole psychological and biological mechanism is not yet fully understood, this diagram may help to give, in a simplified way, a possible explanation of its psychological mechanism. It is taken from a helpful book by the psychiatrist Dr. Rorie.[2]

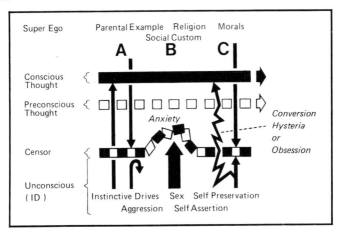

The censor is a shield protecting our personalities from the full force of our instinctive drives, which if they all reached consciousness, would destroy us. It is made up of an acquired element from our environment (our parents' influence, religion, culture and so on), and an inherited element common to all of us.

A represents certain instinctual impulses which are acceptable to the conscious mind and are therefore permitted by the censor to reach consciousness. Others that are unacceptable are repressed and turned back into unconsciousness. Under calm conditions there is an equilibrium and the person is considered to be a healthy, stable individual.

B shows what happens under conditions of stress where the instinctive drives almost break through the censor into consciousness and the person is in a state of anxiety with symptoms such as depression, insomnia and headaches.

C represents a device the mind sometimes adopts to ease the tension. It allows the instinctual impulses into consciousness provided they wear some more acceptable disguise — such as phobias, obsessions or hysteria. When this happens the anxiety and depression are usually diminished.

We are not sure why some people are more prone to this sort of depression than others. It seems that there are two factors: a constitutional one — the material we were born with; and an environmental one — the stress we are subjected to. If we imagine our psychological make-up to be like an elastic band, 'stress' stretches the band until it reaches the limit of its elasticity. Further stretching causes symptoms in the rubber.

Dealing with Depression

Obviously a small band will not stand up to the same amount of stress as a large one. The size of the band represents the constitutional (i.e. inherited) element. Some of us were born with small bands and we have to learn to live within this God-given limitation; others have been given larger bands and can therefore stand up to more of the rough and tumble of life.

It should be emphasised that stress is very rarely caused by circumstances of over-work but by strained relationships between people. We should not ask 'What lies behind these symptoms?' but 'Who?'. The elastic band is relaxed by two conflicting persons changing the circumstances or going away for a holiday.

Guilt and Depression

An example from the genius of Shakespeare may help us to understand these terms.

Lady Macbeth was suffering terribly from guilt feelings for her share in the murder of Banquo, walking restlessly in her sleep, obsessionally washing her hands to rid them of guilt and bloodstains, and crying out: 'What, will these hands ne'er be clean? . . . all the perfume of Arabia will not sweeten this little hand.'

Her husband hoped that the physician would be able to ease these symptoms for her:
'Canst thou not minister to a mind diseased,
Pluck from the memory a rooted sorrow,
Raze out the written troubles of the brain,
And with some sweet oblivious antidote,
Cleanse the stuffed bosom of that perilous stuff
Which weighs upon the heart?'[3]
But the physician some time before had said:
'More needs she the divine than the physician,
God, God forgive us all!'[3]

In some the depression and other psychological symptoms, as with Lady Macbeth, spring from guilty feelings which arise from real unconfessed and unforgiven sin and the remedy is not in some 'oblivious antidote' – a tranquilliser or an anti-depressant – but in the cleansing of the conscience by the blood of Christ. In other cases the symptoms may seem just as bad but there is no real sin that has caused them. The patient is mentally ill and needs expert treatment.

In yet other cases there are exaggerated guilt feelings for a sin that to the counsellor may seem trivial and of little consequence. But he should resist the temptation to ease the conscience by minimising the sin. Rather let him magnify the mercy and love of God and the peace that can come from the blood of the cross.

Feeling guilty (psychological guilt) is not the same as being guilty (legal guilt). It is possible to feel guilty without being guilty and, equally, to be guilty without feeling guilty. To emphasise this important distinction we could call psychological guilt 'moral pain' and legal guilt 'moral disease'. Psychiatry is concerned with the pain; it cannot and should not attempt to treat the disease. If only we would understand this and render to psychiatry the things that are psychological and to God the things that are God's, a great deal of disappointment would be avoided.

Once I saw a young man who described himself as a homosexual, so suffering from the pain of guilt that he had been unable to work for several years. He told me that he had been to a psychiatrist. 'What did he say to you?' I asked. 'He told me that I was expecting too much of psychiatry,' was his sad reply.

Freud called psychological guilt 'a topographic form of anxiety'[4] and said that 'every neurosis masks a certain amount of unconscious sense of guilt'.[5] The apostle John wrote, 'Fear always contains some of the torture of feeling guilty'.[6]

The connection between neurosis and guilt (especially sexual guilt) may often not be fully appreciated even by medical men. When a leader in the British Medical Journal stated that 'sexual promiscuity is debasing to the personalities of those who practise it, fraught with serious dangers, especially to women, and damaging to the interests of society,'[7] a doctor wrote to attack this view as being unacceptable in a scientific magazine 'unless supported by very adequate evidence'. 'Indeed,' he concluded, 'what little evidence that does exist suggests that the contrary view is probably more tenable'.[8]

The Journal was defended by another doctor however, who wrote 'from an experience of more than 40 years of problems of social psychiatry'. While agreeing that promiscuity was not the only cause of sexual neurosis, he wrote: 'The almost certain way to acquire these neuroses (the anxiety-linked, the fixated, the compulsive sexual neuroses, etc.) is to indulge in promiscuity, or in fact to bring the sexual instinct into use in any circumstances divorced from the links of the tender emotions. In sexual maturity the latter emotions supply all the drive of the sexual instinct and at the same time completely circumscribe its use to conditions which are healthy psychologically.'[9]

I was once chatting to someone whose doctor had suggested that she went for psychiatric help. She told me how she had been the victim of terribly tragic circumstances. 'Why, when it wasn't my fault, do I always feel so guilty?' she concluded.

'Were you guilty in any way?' I asked.

She replied sharply, 'Everyone knows that it wasn't my fault.'

'I wasn't trying to accuse you', I said, 'but only trying to help you. My own experience is that I am rarely as innocent as my reason convinces me.'

She began to weep, saying, 'I was guilty and I have ruined my life.'

'No', I replied, 'you haven't ruined it. This is where life begins. Remember how the Pharisees mercilessly exposed the woman they had caught in adultery, accusing her in public before the Lord? She too must have felt that her life had been ruined. I have often wondered why His response was to write in the dust on the Temple floor. It may have been that He was trying to convey to her that even in the dust of a ruined life He has a message of hope to write. When the Pharisees had left He stood up and said to her "I don't blame you. Go and sin no more." He doesn't blame you either,' I added, 'but longs for you to be a guilt-free, happy person.'

'But how?' was her immediate question. In my reply I used this quotation from the New Testament: 'If we refuse to admit that we are sinners, then we live in a world of illusion and truth becomes a stranger to us. But if we freely admit that we have sinned, we find God utterly reliable and straightforward – He forgives our sins and makes us thoroughly clean from all that is evil. For if we take up the attitude "We have not sinned", we flatly deny God's diagnosis of our condition and cut ourselves off from what He has to say to us.'[10]

Weeks later she wrote a moving letter telling of how God had been dealing with her. She and her friends were enjoying a new freedom together. 'Calvary' love (God's forgiving love for her) had replaced the haunting guilt and hidden anxiety that lay at the root of her depression. The Bible expresses this succinctly in the phrase 'Perfect love casts out fear.'[11] She had become conscious of that 'perfect love' of God for her and it had 'cast out' her anxiety.

Loneliness and Depression

'Why am I so lonely when there are over 2,000 here?' The question was carved on a desk in a university lecture room.

I once said to a very depressed patient, 'Tell me in a sentence or two your main trouble.' Slowly and deliberately she answered, 'If I died tonight no one would shed a tear and in a week not a person in the world would ever think of me again.'

An elderly man called me to his bed when I was visiting a medical ward. 'What's the trouble?' I asked.

'I'm so lonely, sir,' was his immediate answer.

In India I thought I saw poverty beyond description. I remember a family settling down in a field near us; children with matchstick legs and arms, teenagers eating grass like animals, parents carrying hollow-eyed starving infants, and grandparents grubbing in the dust for roots; without food, without a roof over their heads, without any material possessions of any kind.

But I had not then worked in London. This Indian family at least cared for one another, they were held together by a strong family bond, their suffering was open and physical. But there are thousands in London who do not belong anywhere, who have never known any affection: parents who never communicate with their children; children who never get through to their parents; lonely wives whose husbands hardly speak to them; widows and pensioners condemned to solitary confinement for the crime of being old; the shy and the ashamed; the bruised and the bewildered. They have no family bonds and the gnawing pains of their hunger are secret and unseen.

In our society we drink and drink at the ocean of our salt-water wealth and then die of thirst. Yet we call ourselves 'the haves' and talk about helping the 'have-nots'. What blindness. There is no greater poverty than the poverty caused by the lack of that warm, outgoing, caring, concern for one another which the apostles called agape. We used to call it 'love' until that word became so debased as to be meaningless. Without it every Christian church or group is a cup without water, a body without a heart. Our whole society is sick with this terrible deficiency of which drug addiction, sexual promiscuity, alcoholism, delinquency and depression are symptoms.

Despair and Depression

Mood-swings between elation and gloom are common. If they are extreme we refer to the condition as cyclothymia, because of the cyclical nature of these moods, which alternate between a bouncing euphoria and an apathetic depression. But we all experience in some degree these changes. In some they are so marked as to present a medical problem, in others so slight as to make them rather dull, flat personalities.

We must learn to know ourselves, and to be what we are, and not to try to force ourselves into another mould or pretend to be what we are not. Living with our moods is better than trying to change our personalities. The mountains of euphoria can be cultivated so that they do not grow the wild bushes of a hearty, garrulous manner which makes us difficult to live with. Instead we may cultivate 'a cheerful heart' which is 'a good medicine'. Equally the valleys of depression need to be drained of the swamps of self-pity, grumbling and pessimistic despair, and planted with the corn of an outgoing care for others.

We must not mistake joy for happiness or despair for depression. Joy is a fruit of the Spirit. It is the opposite of boredom, emptiness and the punctured life which has lost all its child-like bounce and resilience, the opposite, in fact, of despair. It is not an emotion but an attitude to life. It does not depend on our inherited personalities but on our spiritual walk and fellowship with Jesus Christ. Similarly there is a difference between depression and despair. Depression is the heart crying out for 'Calvary' love, despair the devil telling us to abandon hope.

Here are some tips which may help to keep depression from turning into despair.

– Find someone in need to visit and help.

– Do not blame or despise yourself; for God does not, and you are of infinite importance to Him.

– Do not hate yourself but be kind to yourself, for God loves you and will never treat you harshly or unkindly.

– Do not nurse self-pity or cherish hurt pride or call them by any other name.

– Do not hide your troubles and failures but express them aloud in words to God, to yourself and to your friends.

– Do not isolate yourself but plan ahead to be sociable and keep to what you planned. 'God sets the solitary in families'.

– Learn to lean on others and do not call independence a virtue; they will lean on you later.

– In your 'up' times put capital into your spiritual bank; find words from the Bible that may help you, people that will encourage you, pleasures that you enjoy, and a church where you feel at home.

– Never neglect your physical health, especially sleep and exercise.

– Learn to relax physically by relaxing tense muscles, when driving, for example; mentally by relaxing tense situations by reconciliation and a willingness to apologise;

and spiritually by coming to Christ, which is faith, and resting, which is trust. (There are a number of paper-backs available on the subject of relaxation).
  — Think much of Calvary, especially the infinite love of God for you personally — tailor-made to fit you and your circumstances exactly.

Depression and Hope

A young scientist once came to see me, suffering from insomnia. 'Are you worried about your exams?' I asked.
  'No, not my exams,' he said. 'I suppose I am a fool to worry, but everyone in our course seems thrilled about the recent advances in technology that can bring a nuclear war-head down from outer space on to any city in the world. I didn't take up my training for that,' he went on. 'I wanted to help people, not destroy them.'

'How happy are those who mourn,' Christ said, 'for they will be comforted.' By this He, meant that the mourner would receive an inner help to deal with what troubles him. This comfort comes by a maturing process. At first he sees the failures of society most clearly; then he begins to discover the same defects in his own group, and even in his family circle; until finally he realises the seeds are all there in his own heart. It is as though he were moving down a via dolorosa whose converging walls bring him to that lonely hill where the mourner stands alone and says, 'Mine were the sufferings He bore, mine the sorrows He carried . . . He was pierced through for my faults, crushed for my sins . . . The Lord laid on Him the burden of my guilt.'[12]
  Is his depression then cured? There is an Arab proverb which says, 'Where the sun always shines there is desert,' and the Bible says, 'The clouds are the dust of His feet'.[13] It is in the dust of our failure that we see His footprints and find a new hope.

  'There was a time when I wouldn't admit what a sinner I was. But my dishonesty made me miserable and filled my days with frustration.
  All day and all night Your hand was heavy on me. My strength evaporated like water on a sunny day.
  Until I finally admitted all my sins to You and stopped trying to hide them. I said to myself, "I will confess them to the Lord." And You forgave me. All my guilt is gone.
  After this experience, I say that every believer should confess his sins to God as soon as he becomes aware of them, while there is yet time to be forgiven. If he does, judgement will not touch him.
  You are my hiding place from every storm of life; You even keep me from getting into trouble. You surround me with songs of victory.

I will instruct you (says the Lord) and guide you along the best pathway for your life; I will advise you and watch your progress.

Don't be like a senseless horse or mule that has to have a bit in its mouth to keep it in line.

Many sorrows come to the wicked, but abiding love surrounds those who trust in the Lord.

So rejoice in Him, all those who are His, and shout for joy, all those who try to obey Him.'[14]

Notes:

1   H.J.Eysenck, 'Fact and Fiction in Psychology'. Pelican
2   D.A.P. Rorie, 'Do Something about those Nerves'. Tandem Press
3   Macbeth. Act V
4   Sigmund Freud, 'Collected Papers', vol. 1. Hogarth Press, p. 125
5   Sigmund Freud, 'Civilisation and its discontents'. Hogarth Press, p. 132
6   1 John 4:17, (J.B. Phillips' translation)
7   British Medical Journal, 25 March, 1967, p. 711
8   British Medical Journal, 30 May, 1967, p. 511
9   British Medical Journal, 10 June, 1967, p. 701
10 1 John 1:5-9, J.B. Phillips
11 1 John 4:18
12 Isaiah 53:4-6
13 Nahum 1:3
14 Psalm 32 from 'Living Psalms and Proverbs'. Tyndale House, Publishers

Learning that Language

An article by David Bendor-Samuel
International Literacy Co-ordinator – Wycliffe Bible Translators

If you expect to be serving abroad for only a limited period, it may seem a waste of time to try to learn the local language. You probably don't expect to become really fluent before you return home, and there will be so many other things which seem to offer a greater return for the work involved. So you may be surprised to learn that there are some very good reasons why you should give time to language learning, however short you expect your stay abroad to be.

Why you should learn that language

The most obvious reason, of course, is so that the message you go to share will be understood. Even in these days when so many people can speak some English, it remains true that to be really effective in talking about spiritual things we must speak the heart language of our hearers. The English they know may be sufficient for business purposes, but observe what language they use for intimate matters which affect beliefs and attitudes. We cannot risk misunderstanding and distortion, and we want them to be free to think about the implications of our message, not struggling to understand it.

But since in a limited stay you may not expect to reach the point of fluent witnessing, consider some reasons of a different kind. You might not realise it, but it is a fact that learning a person's language (rather than talking to him in your own) signals some very important things about your attitude to him and his culture. It shows appreciation of his value as a person and a member of a developing nation. It demonstrates that you are moving toward him, not demanding that he move toward you. It emphasises that the

Gospel is not just a 'western' religion, but can be given expression in any language. If we make no attempt to learn their language, then we are in fact signalling just the reverse of these things, and should not be surprised if we return home feeling that we never really 'made contact' with them at any deep level.

In a short stay, your attitudes will be of much greater significance than what you say or even what you do. So even if you don't make rapid progress, do not despair; the fact that you tried will count for a great deal. It will also open the door to relationships with people outside the strict confines of your job, e.g. entry into their homes and social occasions. This will be a rewarding experience, and also enable you to understand their cultural values much better as you seek to witness.

Problems you will encounter

Though language learning is so important and so rewarding, do not expect it to be easily achieved (unless you are one of those rare people who have a natural flair for languages). Here are some of the difficulties which most of us must expect to face.

Slow progress may make you discouraged – you feel you'll never be able to talk freely! That's just a fact you'll have to learn to live with; after all, you didn't make much progress with English during your first two years of trying! To keep on trying is the important thing, and to add a little more each day.

Pressure of other work and a natural desire to spend time on things which seem to give quick results, will certainly bother you. The answer here is a careful setting of priorities for the time you have available (check with longer-term workers as to how important getting some of the language really is) and then a little self-discipline. Remember how easily the good can become the enemy of the best, and try to form a picture of your total impact as a person in the situation.

Another problem may be the impression you get while at your work, that everyone really speaks English adequately. This is quite unlikely to hold good outside the narrow limits of your work situation, for very few people are thoroughly bilingual: and it is in the non-work situation that many of your best opportunities for the Lord will occur – if you can only take advantage of them. After all, they will assume that you are being paid to be there doing that work(!), but what you do in your spare time will show them where your true interests lie.

Probably your greatest problems will lie in knowing just how to go about learning that language, unless you are fortunate enough to be working with an organisation that gives you practical help in this area. So how can you help yourself? Well, the Summer Institute of Linguistics runs a 6-week course every summer geared especially for people who are going to have to help themselves learn a language in a missionary situation. Six weeks may seem a long time, but it is an investment that will pay rich dividends. If you cannot take such a course, then at least try one of the books which has been written especially for people in your situation. For details of what is available see below. Don't insist on 're-inventing the wheel' – take advantage of the experience of others, it will make a tremendous difference.

Learning that Language

Some practical suggestions

As these books and courses will tell you, learning a second language is not primarily a matter of memorising long vocabulary lists and confusing irregular constructions out of a grammar book! Language learning is primarily a question of acquiring a new set of habits and reactions – something like learning to drive a car! Learning things by heart still has a place, but it must be done in such a way as to help you acquire those new habits, and much learning takes place best as you expose yourself to situations in which the language is used and as you make contact with the life and culture of the people. Careful listening and willingness to mimic and be laughed at, are as important as memory drills, and much more fun! More than anything else, your progress will be the outworking of your attitudes to the new language and the people who speak it – which is why you need to start to learn even for a stay of a month or two.

You must expect to find some unfamiliar sounds which may be difficult for you at first. Be of good cheer, however. If you keep trying, you will master these before long, just as every child does – provided that is, that you are willing to keep on being corrected (and can find friends willing to help you!) Differences in the sounds will probably include some strange consonants or vowels. More important, however, are the more subtle differences of tone (syllables being pronounced at different pitch levels to give a different meaning) and of intonation (the tune of the sentence as a whole). Because English does not use tone to distinguish otherwise similar words, we find it hard to hear this in another language, but do not kid yourself that you are tone deaf – unless, that is, you cannot hear the difference between "Tom is asleep" and "Tom is asleep?" (rising tone on the question being the distinction). If you listen carefully and keep on trying, you will eventually hear such differences and the books will tell you how to help yourself.

Then there will be differences of grammatical pattern – the way the parts of sentences are put together. You can expect to find a different order of words, such as "kill man tiger lake by will plural" (the man will kill tigers by the lake). There may be affixes or inflections added to all the words in a phrase (he bought two-a little-a black-a kittens-a) or unexpected ways of saying things (I go come). Very likely there will be little words or pieces of words which don't seem to mean anything, and seem unpredictable in their occurrence to us (but not to them!). Here is where the memory drills really come in useful, helping you form new habits of speech so that the words will naturally 'come out right' as you speak, without your having to consciously think about their order or their affixes. Here again, a book on language learning will prove invaluable.

You will want to learn a few new words of vocabulary each day, especially at first. (Later, struggling through a local newspaper will bring you lots of new words and idioms, besides helping you understand how people think.) Concentrate on words that you will be able to use in your life situation, for using words helps you remember them. You will also want to learn by heart useful phrases such as greetings, questions, imperatives, conversation openers and sustainers (it's amazing how useful the latter are for giving the impression you have understood, and so stopping the conversation from grinding to a halt!) So do set yourself up with lists of things to learn (a good pedagogical grammar will do this for you) and do use the words as you learn them. A few at a time, and put to use straight away – that's the way to beat memory fatigue.

Above all, do remember that languages are learned as people try to speak them! So don't give up, all embarrassed, when you make a mistake, and do allocate time each day, not only to learning and drilling, but also to being in an informal situation where you can listen and try to enter conversation. In a short term, it's not the progress you make that counts so much as whether or not you make the attempt, and the Lord is able to bless your efforts far beyond their desert, in this as in everything else.

Helps available

Courses

The Summer Institute of Linguistics offers a six-week 'Basic Course' in language-learning. It is held near High Wycombe, Bucks, starting early July every year. For details write SIL, Horsleys Green, Stokenchurch, Bucks, HP14 3XL.

If you will be learning a major world language, there may be courses, or teach-yourself book-and-recording courses available commercially. Enquire from the mission with which you will be working.

Books on the principles of language learning

LAMP ('Language Acquisition Made Practical – sub-titled Field methods for Language Learners'), by ET & ES Brewster. This is the latest, the best and, of course, the most expensive! Very attractively produced, clear, practical and easy to use. Published 1976 by Lingua House, 915 West Jackson, Colorado Springs, Colorado 80907, U.S.A. 384pp $8.95.

'Becoming Bilingual – a guide to language learning', by D.N. Larson and W.A. Smalley. An excellent and practical volume, but rather more technical than LAMP, and not so attractively produced. Published 1972, and available from William Carey Library, 533 Hermosa St., South Pasadena, California 91030, U.S.A. 426pp. Priced around $6 or $7.

'Learning a Foreign Language', by E.A. Nida. A standard textbook for years, but geared more to analysis and with less attention to practical drills, which have been much developed in more recent works. 3rd edition published 1957. Available from Friendship Press, P.O. Box 37844, Cincinnati, Ohio 45237, U.S.A. 212pp $4.50.

Each of these books are very good value; do get one!

Personal Relationships

An Open Letter

from Dr Marion Ashton

Dear...

Will you put your name in there, you who are preparing to go out for a short term of service? I want to speak to you personally on the subject of relationships and much that I say will apply in principle to you whoever you are, man or woman, married or single. What I say may sound theoretical but you must turn it into practice when you get to your sphere of work, according to your own particular need and personality.

It is a great privilege that you are being given this opportunity. It will above all be an opportunity to learn. To learn much about yourself, about others of different nationalities, about another land and culture, about God's work and God's ways. Will you make it your intention to be a learner from start to finish? Not quick to make judgements, not quick to decide what is wrong and what ought to be done, but always with a mind open to learn. If that is your attitude it will make a big difference to all your relationships.

I want first to talk about stress because it is stress that affects our relationships more than anything else. You are going to have big adjustments to make. You will have to adjust to a new climate, a new culture, new work, new standards, new living conditions, new relationships, not only with nationals but with the team with which you are to work, which will probably include those from different countries. It is one thing to adjust to changes when we are reasonably secure and sure of ourselves; it is much more difficult when we are feeling insecure and unsure as you will almost certainly be when you first go out. In all probability in the homeland you have been reasonably secure emotionally; you have known what it is to have a significance of your own, giving a right sense of worth and self-respect; you have felt you belonged; you have felt accepted and needed. These are some of the things that make for emotional security, and until you find them again in the new sphere you are likely to feel insecure and unsure of yourself. We need time to make these kind of adjustments. The shorter the span of time in which they have to be made the more stress it puts upon us and the more likely we are to feel frustration. As a short term worker you are bound to have some feeling that the time is short, so you must adjust as quickly as possible, if you are to give a useful contribution. All this amounts to a stressful situation. Inside yourself you may experience an insecurity, a lack of confidence and a type of frustration which you have never experienced before.

Will you accept that the situation is bound to be one of stress? You are going to be under pressure within and without! That stress or pressure will have a great effect on your relationships. It will produce dangers and difficulties in relationships, but at the same time you can learn to find in relationships the greatest help in coping with stress and in becoming a more mature person.

Before thinking of specific relationships let us think about two things which can have a positive effect on your relationships with others and with your circumstances: —

Commitment

One of the secrets of stability, one of the secrets of giving one's best, one of the secrets of developing helpful relationships is to commit oneself fully to the present. There is a danger in short term service of thinking that it is not worth getting really dug in to the work, it is not worth making really meaningful relationships, it is not worth thinking seriously about learning the language because you are not going to be in the work for long. I suggest that it is a Christian principle and therefore a very practical one that you commit yourself totally to 'today', regardless of whether the situation will last few days or many days. Commit yourself totally in loyalty to the missionary society under whose auspices you are working. Submit to its authority as you would if you were a full member. Reckon that you belong to it. Commit yourself to your fellow-workers to accept them, to learn from them, to make good relationships with them. Commit yourself to the work as if it is to be your life's work. (How do you know that it's not!) Commit yourself to learn as much as you can about the culture, customs and language of the people to whom you have been sent. This is much more satisfying than a very superficial commitment based on the shortness of the time. It will also help in the process of adjustment, because we never adjust to that to which we do not commit ourselves.

Physical Well-being

It is much more difficult to cope with stress if we are below par physically. We all know how much more easily we get irritable, or sorry for ourselves, or discouraged if we are very tired. Grievances are much more likely to get exaggerated and relationships to go wrong. Please take seriously your physical well-being. Listen to what others tell you about the need for extra rest when you go to the tropics, (if it is to the tropics you are going). Be humble enough to do what is suggested and take the midday siesta. Ask the Lord to guide you in getting a right balance between work and rest. Learn to accept your own limitations and not to be always competing with others who may be stronger or may have lived much longer in the place you are in.

Rest is not just cessation of activity, it is change of activity, so try to plan ahead for recreational activity. Have you got a hobby? What about music? Are you taking some light literature? I remember a great missionary saint when staying with us in Africa taking "Three men in a boat" out of our bookcase for a Sunday afternoon rest! If you have to use English in the work and will have little opportunity to learn the national language, perhaps learning that could be a hobby. Pray about this; the Lord wants you to be your best and recreation is vital to physical well-being.

It is easy in certain places and types of work to get slack about one's appearance. Reasonable care is a help towards self-respect.

Now let us think about your relationships with others. I am going to say something about your relationship with authority, with fellow team members and with nationals, but first I want to mention something that applies to all these relationships. It is that under stress all our reactions tend to be greatly exaggerated. If when you are upset you tend to become aggressive, under stress you may, to your horror, find yourself actually losing your temper. If on the other hand you tend to withdraw somewhat, you may find yourself becoming so withdrawn that your silent mood becomes very difficult for others to cope with. If you tend to find it difficult to take criticism, under stress you may find that even imagined criticism becomes a threat and leaves you with an awful sense of failure and inferiority. If you tend to be irritated by certain habits or idiosyncracies in others, under stress you may find yourself unbearably irritated by very small things. And so I could go on. This may all sound very depressing but if you go out as a learner it can be a wonderful opportunity for change. To see our reactions in an exaggerated form need not lead us to disappointment in ourselves and discouragement and a guilty sense of failure; it can lead us, for the first time to face our reactions and the effect they have on others, and to ask God to show us the pathway by which they can be changed.

Relationship to Authority

Here is your opportunity to learn to submit to authority! It is not likely to be one authority but a number of different authorities. The authority of the mission at home, the authority of the field leaders, the authority of the local church, the civil authority of the country into which you go. It is very unlikely that you will not inwardly rebel against some aspect of these different authorities, especially when there seems no point to some of the regulations imposed on you. Can you make submission without criticism your aim? If you do and wait long enough you will probably find that there are reasons behind many things which at first you thought were unreasonable. Discrediting of authority is very infectious and very destructive. Don't do it!

Relationship with Fellow Team Members

Your relationship with these may be more difficult than with nationals. You will be thrown closely together and will not be able to escape from difficult relationships as easily as you can in the homeland. You will very probably come from very different backgrounds and different countries even if English is the mother tongue of all of you. Remembering what I said about exaggerated reactions, how are you going to react when what you think of as reasonable British reserve is interpreted as superiority? Are you going to hold to it that our ways must be best, even to driving on the left of the road, and having a certain kind of table-manners? We do still tend to give others the feeling that we think ourselves a superior race! Perhaps you are going to see a wonderful opportunity to learn to get rid of pride of race and to accept others as they are and to appreciate the very ways in which they differ from you. If you are to settle down and find that feeling of belonging and of being accepted and being needed in the new sphere a lot depends on you going out actively to commit yourself to the team. You want to feel accepted, start by positively accepting them. If you can bring yourself to share any of your early problems with others and find prayer fellowship, that will be a tremendous help.

Relationship with Nationals

Inasmuch as most of these will probably not speak English, one of the greatest difficulties will be communication. This can cause frustration and a sense of isolation and uselessness. But you can learn ways of communicating without words, such as gestures to make, gestures to avoid. Perhaps the most important attitude to pray for is one of respect. Respect for their different ways and customs, respect for their different standards, respect for their different sense of humour, respect for what they accept or do not accept

in relationships between those of different sexes. Respect will result in sensitiveness towards them which is surely an important part of love. It is very healthy to have to face up to things in ourselves which certain other races do not accept. We all react in certain ways under stress and tend to expect others to accept that that is just the way we are! "That's just me" we say, "people should understand." Possibly the commonest is, under stress, to 'jump' on people, to speak abruptly, to raise our voices. What a shock it is to find that we cannot get away with 'that's just me'! We have got to find God's way of changing or we shall never be acceptable.

Relationship with God

Lastly, let me talk about your relationship with God. Your relationship with God through Jesus Christ is the one utterly secure, stable and central relationship of your life. Make much of it! Even when you feel insecure as far as human relationships are concerned you can know your worth to God as a unique individual; think much about that! You can know that He accepts you just as you are, you belong to Him; think much about that! You can know that He needs you, you have a work to do in His Kingdom which only you can do; thank Him for that! Think about these things particularly when you are feeling discouraged and insignificant.

Don't let disappointment, disillusionment, discouragement lead to self-condemnation and so to spoiling your fellowship with God. Keep open communication with Him remembering that there is no condemnation to those that are in Christ Jesus. Rest your heart on the fact that God has sent you out, He has commissioned you, therefore He will be your sufficiency. In 2 Cor.1 and 3 we find that Paul rested his heart on these things when he was under pressure.

These reactions we have thought about can be changed because the Lord Jesus does actually live in you. He is changing you all the way through your Christian life so you do not need to despair of ever being different. No doubt you will have feelings of frustration, resentment, self-pity and other negative emotions. The thing that matters is what you do with those emotions when they come. If you pretend that they are not there or if you entertain them and nurse them, you will either go down the pathway of blaming yourself and becoming full of guilty feelings of inadequacy and failure, or you will blame others and succumb to the miserable mood of discontent and criticism. Both these pathways are destructive to yourself and will lead to widening gaps between you and others, and clouding of your fellowship with the Lord. If on the other hand you acknowledge them openly to the Lord, not taking the line, "I'm a Christian, I ought not to feel like this," but being real about your emotions and saying "Lord, this is what I feel, please handle these emotions for me," then you will increasingly experience the truth of 1 John 1:7 "If we walk in the light, as He is in the light, we have fellowship with one another, and the blood of Jesus His Son cleanses us from all sin." This will result in richer fellowship with God and better relationships with fellow workers. You will find forgiveness instead of condemnation, and gradually you will find that He is handling and changing your emotions.

Do try to guard jealously your times alone with God and with His Word; nothing can substitute for that. It is in the quiet, beholding the glory of the Lord, as well as in all the stressful circumstances, that the Lord does His changing work. 2 Cor. 3:18.

It always comforts me that Paul had to learn. In Phil. 4:11 and 12 he says, talking of 'any and all circumstances', "I have learned in whatever state I am, to be content." There is no greater lesson you could learn in all your relationships and circumstances in your time overseas!

P.S.

All that I have said applies to you all but there are two special areas of relationships which I have not mentioned and which ought to be thought about and recognised as potential areas of stress. The first relates to married couples. Don't be surprised if the stress of adjustments produces strain within your marriage relationship. Do try to give one another time and above all do keep communicating with one another. The second relates to single workers of both sexes. You will have had all the natural feelings and desires towards marriage and you may have had real dealings with the Lord on this subject. Don't be surprised if these come up again, even in an exaggerated form, when you go overseas. Don't condemn yourself, but do guard against their leading you into hasty and unwise relationships.

Suggested books: –

Any by Dr Paul Tournier. S.C.M. Press
Especially: 'Escape from loneliness'
                'The strong and the weak'
                'The person reborn'

'Our rebel emotions', by Bernard Mobbs. Hodder and Stoughton

'Run and not be weary', by Dr D.L. Carlson. Lakeland

'Prescription for anxiety', Leslie Weatherhead. Hodder and Stoughton.

Christian Conduct Overseas

Two contrasting statements, outlining the principles to be considered, for those living in situations of conflict.

1 Christian Conduct in Situations of Conflict

A statement of guidelines by the Council of Mennonite Mission Board Secretaries, Mennonite Central Committee, Council of Mennonite Colleges and Council of Mennonite Seminaries in the USA.

The World, the Disciple and the Kingdom

The World Situation

Although all of human history has been marked by violence, it is in contemporary times that man's violence against man has reached unprecedented proportions. This is manifested in various ways:

1 The unrelenting efforts of nations to apply the most advanced technology and knowledge to weaponry and systems of destruction.

2 The bewildering change brought about in human society through an ever-accelerating scientific revolution.

3 The collapse of old social and political systems (e.g. colonialism) due to inward decay and moral culpability.

4 The impact of a new quest for self-determination by the downtrodden peoples and nations of the world.

Realism requires that we view the basic human condition for what it is – a personal and collective rebellion against God. The finest and highest achievements of man are continually subverted and perverted by being turned against the common good and to the purposes of selfish men and groups. In short the world is that place where the "rule of God" has yet to be recognised and accepted. Those persons and structures which do not follow the will of God will inevitably be under the domination of evil and the demonic.

The Disciple's Calling

The disciple is called to be a messenger. His witness is that there is "good news" for mankind. It is his privilege to proclaim that the power of evil can be overwhelmed and defeated and men can be liberated from the tyranny of violence by the power of the resurrection of Jesus Christ. The disciple witnesses as a citizen of the Kingdom of God. His loyalty to this Kingdom and its King must be unconditional. The mode of his witness is modelled after that of the King Himself, Jesus Christ. In the incarnation Jesus identified fully with man in order that He might reveal the Father perfectly. The incarnation above all else meant the rejection of resort to violent retaliation when confronted by the forces of evil. Instead Jesus took the form of a servant, accepted the way of the cross knowingly and willingly, thereby defeating the power of death and the demonic. It is this pattern of servanthood which is normative for the disciple.

It is the call of the disciple to live with the tension of the "already" and the "not yet", the eschatological awareness of the ultimate triumph of God's kingdom in confrontation with this age which is not yet finally subdued. It is this eschatological awareness which informs the disciple's ethical response to the world.

The Perspective of the Kingdom

The message of Jesus was that the kingdom of God has come and that God's rule — with its implications for justice, righteousness and peace — has begun. The coming of the kingdom of God signals hope for man.

The kingdom therefore points to the new thing that God is doing, bringing all things to completion in Jesus Christ. One important feature of this new creation is that it transcends the boundaries and barriers men have erected against each other. The Biblical vision depicts the gathering together of men from all backgrounds in a new community under a new confession: Jesus is Lord.

A second feature of this new creation is that it results from the missionary response of God's people. The mission is to the nations, to the peoples of the world. It requires a supreme loyalty to Jesus as Lord; the call of God's people is to be agents of reconciliation "on Christ's behalf". It is a vision and task which places all other considerations of national or ethnic loyalties, social status or even personal security under its prior claim.

The Relationships of the Overseas Worker

Though the Christian worker professes in his commitments and values the Kingdom of God and strives to incarnate in his style of life the universality of this Kingdom, he is also a member of a variety of groups whose relationships are frequently in tension with the Kingdom of God. Because of these relationships the overseas worker will recognize that all of his actions implicate the persons and organizations with which he associates. It is unrealistic to think that he retains his private identity.

A crucial issue is the way in which the worker identifies in his new context. The effectiveness of his service depends on achieving genuine rapport with church and community. On the other hand, his true value will be limited if he loses his capacity for constructive but critical evaluation. In addition it should be noted that the reason for not seeking total identification is not because neutrality is the ideal stance but rather that it is impossible to become an agent of reconciliation apart from an ethically independent position. To give substance to this intention there should be programme efforts designed to work actively toward this evangelical goal of effecting reconciliation.

To the Local Church

The primary relationship of each worker on the field is to the local fellowship of believers. As much as possible, the overseas worker should enter fully into the life and work of the local church in the area where he is assigned, thus giving visible expression to the unity of believers and the universality of the Church.

One who is affiliated with a local church overseas normally enjoys the same rights and privileges as any other member of the church, unless these rights and privileges have been modified by congregational policy or by the laws of the country. There may be instances where freedom of religion and expression granted to a citizen is denied an expatriate.

The overseas worker should be informed about the issues and problems which affect the life of the people with whom he is working. His involvement in their struggles will be determined to a certain degree by the laws and customs of the country in which he works and the attitude and judgment of national colleagues and church leaders.

The overseas worker should also bear in mind that the church has far too often allied itself with political and social leaders who perpetuate injustice and support privilege for the few. When the worker finds this to be the situation he must seek to challenge the church to a sense of righteousness and justice. If he fails he must decide in what manner he can exercise his conscience or adjust to the situation. There may be occasions when workers will remove themselves from unjust circumstances or face expulsion as a witness of conscience.

Where there is injustice and oppression, the worker will feel inclined to identify with the oppressed, the poor and the imprisoned. (Luke 4:18–19). The ministry of reconciliation compels us to strive to overcome evil with good; to support the things which make for peace and to work to end the conflicts which rend our world. The concerned worker will not only exercise his conscience regarding evil, but will use means for exercising this conscience appropriate to the way of Christ and constantly challenge the church to its responsibility.

In recent times the church, particularly those bodies relating to overseas communions through mission and service agencies, has frequently had its activities proscribed. We regret such developments which may indeed be judgments on the church's failure to be authentically responsive to the context in which it exists. On the other hand there is no reason for us to expect an easy, comfortable existence for the church. Whatever the case, the local worker should not allow difference of political ideology to be the primary basis for decision making.

To the Sending Church

A second relationship is to the sending organisation or church. It is the sending group which commissions the worker and provides various kinds of support. The worker will want, to the extent possible, to keep the sending group informed as to his whereabouts and the general situation and to enlist their moral and prayer support.

It is the responsibility of the sponsoring group to demonstrate its support and confidence in both the worker and the local church or Christian fellowship with whom the worker associates by vesting in them the responsibility for making any decisions in a time of crisis regarding the temporary re-assignment or relocation of the worker. This confidence is justified by the faith that the "two or three" gathered under the Spirit's blessing will be guided in their search for the will of God in difficult circumstances. While we are concerned for the safety of all God's people, we very much believe that God's people are in truth strangers and pilgrims in this world and that the cross we are called to bear will include suffering and even death.

To the Host Country

The overseas worker will recognize that he does not carry the rights of citizenship in a country other than his own and that the peoples of most countries will want to form their own government and their own life style. He will avoid imposing his own ideology or culture on the people whom he serves.

As a resident of a foreign country, the worker will respect the government's laws and regulations particularly as they relate to alien registration, taxes, customs, monetary exchange, permits for travel and licences of various kinds. Good judgment, tactfulness and Christian grace should be demonstrated at all times in contacts with government officials. Because of the danger of misinterpretation, caution should be used in making statements, especially written, that criticise or reflect on government policies and activities, living standards, cultural practices, or educational levels.

The overseas worker should realize that his movements and attitudes, expressed and unexpressed, are under constant surveillance. In areas of tension and conflict the civilian or military governmental authorities may maintain censorship of all incoming and outgoing mail. It is necessary, therefore, to be prudent and use good judgment in writing official and personal letters about local and national political situations in the country where one is serving. The same is true for what is kept as part of the local files and records.

Since the Christian is concerned with the total needs of man, both individually and socially, an overseas worker will be concerned with the political, economic and social issues confronting the host country. He will recognise that it is impossible to maintain a truly neutral stance. However, as an expatriate, it will be expected and may be specifically required, that he abstain from political involvements. In all situations the counsel and advice of the church leaders is to be sought and duly respected.

To the Sending Country

The overseas worker should avoid giving the impression that his primary loyalty, either politically or culturally belongs to his homeland and to the diplomatic, commercial, or military representatives of that homeland in his field of service. He will be especially sensitive to the appearance of preferring to shop or to socialise in contexts related to his homeland. As a citizen of the Kingdom of Heaven he knows that all people are embraced by God's love and concern and looks forward to the time when the whole creation will be brought to unity in Christ. He will express the conditional nature of all national attachments both verbally and in his attitude and life style.

The worker thus need not feel compelled to be a defender of his homeland and its government, "right or wrong". Where his home government does take a stand for what is right and seeks to help other nations in their struggle for liberty and justice, he can be grateful, and participate, according to his abilities and availability, in these efforts. But, as sometimes happens, if his government has policies and practices which support the oppressor, he should not fear to affirm that this government like all governments, stands under the judgment of God for its misuse of power. He should not fear expressing his concerns about such policies, according to the dictates of his convictions and conscience.

Principles of Action during Open Hostilities

Throughout the history of Christendom, Christ's servants have worked in the midst of danger and conflict and have often risked personal security to be obedient to their calling and assignment. Today, overseas workers live and minister in countries which may at times experience unrest, civil war, or other types of danger, hostility and conflict.

Occasions may arise where the Gospel is on trial and the worker directly involved. In such situations he is to follow the example of Jesus, Who refused to retaliate or defend Himself and on the cross prayed for the forgiveness of His enemies.

In times of crises there are no easy answers for the overseas workers who try to fulfil their responsibility. It may be possible to continue one's work even though the rest of the world, through propaganda and sensational publicity, may deem the situation impossible.

Consult the Local Church

In any consideration of actions in an emergency, the interest of the local Christian church must be paramount. The process by which this is ascertained is very important. A genuine effort must be made to get the true feelings of the church and not just polite answers. This may require consulting a variety of people. The decision of a worker to remain and share in a dangerous situation with a local Christian group may strengthen and encourage that community. Conversely, the presence of expatriates may be an embarrassment or even a cause for reprisals against the nationals. Therefore a worker should not selfishly decide that he will remain at any cost. On the other hand, it may be very difficult for workers to return with the respect and goodwill of the church after a total evacuation if the church or local group did not share in the feeling that the evacuation was urgent.

Search for Means to End Hostilities

In conflict situations the worker must take care not to identify with any particular local faction or point of view at the expense of other people's. Rather, there should be concern for reaching understanding and meeting human needs on both sides of a conflict. The worker should strive to be a spokesman for peace and reconciliation, seeking for clarification and discussion of the issues causing the conflict. He must urge the renunciation of violence or the use of violence in any form, in settling disputes.

Bind up the Wounds of the Suffering

In the midst of conflict there are almost always persons who will need food, medicine and shelter. Workers should use these opportunities to show the love of God in the midst of distress. In such situations, due caution should be exercised to assure safety and security, but personal safety should never be the sole factor in making decisions. On the other hand, it should also be remembered that life is given by God to each individual and is therefore a sacred trust. To carelessly or thoughtlessly endanger one's own life or the life or lives of others is not necessarily a Christian witness.

Contact Government Officials

Local government officials should be contacted and due consideration given their opinions in making plans and decision. Orders of the legally constituted local government to leave the country should usually be obeyed.

Workers may also want to keep in touch with their own consulates and officials. It should be remembered that consulates tend to exercise considerable caution because they are responsible for the safety of their citizens. They may advise but they cannot command. It is worth remembering that consulates make decisions on the basis of their own nation's interests rather than on a Christian or humanitarian basis. If a worker refuses the advice of his consulate he should realise that he thereby assumes personal responsibility for his own safety. Sometimes the consulate of another country may have better insights into the situation than that of the home country.

To leave or not to leave?

This is the last issue to be faced during an emergency. The normal stance of an overseas worker will be to fulfil his commitment to the church and community in which he resides. Danger in itself is not necessarily a cause for evacuation. The act of staying or leaving in itself is an important indication to the local church and community of one's sense of mission and identification.

In a conflict situation the decision to remain or leave should be arrived at only after the fullest possible consultation with the local Christian group and agency co-workers. It is usually preferable that decisions be arrived at corporately. However, due consideration must be given to regional or local differences which render a uniform decision for all workers impossible. Some consideration will be given to children and women and the ages of the persons involved. There are also differences of style and gift among persons that make some more competent in stress situations than others. In any case, every effort should be made to respect the decisions reached by the group or individuals in it concerning staying or leaving.

The decision to leave does not imply a return to the homeland. Normally the workers will travel to the neighbouring country to await further instructions from the sending agency. Throughout the process workers will be expected to try to remain in communication with the sending agency but no unnecessary risks should be taken simply to fulfil this obligation.

The worker should thus find it possible to move without being fearful of the work collapsing because of his absence. In a similar way the worker is not expected to be so preoccupied with property that he would find it necessary to risk life or safety for its protection.

We expect the Christian worker will even in such situations "seek first His Kingdom and His righteousness" as a testimony of hope and confidence rather than the panic of fear.

2 A Statement of Position

An Open Letter from a Group of Catholic and Protestant Missionaries in the Republic of Korea to Fellow Missionary Colleagues
From International Review of Mission, April 1976

The following letter is an effort to clarify to ourselves and to others the reasons, both personal and theological, on which we base our actions. It is a statement of our position and the interpretation of our role as Christian missionaries in the Republic of Korea at this particular time and in these particular circumstances in the history of this country.

As Christians and missionaries we are all a part of a common community, though representing differing opinions and ways of practising our common mission. In light of these diversities we offer this letter as an effort to share our particular understanding of the Scriptures that has led us to our present position. We trust that these expressions will be accepted in the spirit of trust and love in which they are offered and, although we do not anticipate complete agreement with our point of view, we would hope that at least a door will remain open between our conflicting understandings.

We realise that many of you already understand this position and may even be in sympathy with our point of view, but there are others who do not and who feel that our stand on certain issues has caused inconveniences to some members of the foreign missionary community. We address this letter to all of you who may be interested.

"With all Christians we share the conviction that the practice of the Christian life must be consistent with the teachings of Scripture. It is our belief that the forms of witness we have been engaged in are in harmony with and indeed are required by these teachings. Though it is not possible in this limited space to provide a full thesis, our understanding of Scripture (the Bible) which provides the rationale for a so-called "political" witness, may be generally summarised as follows:

We believe that the ultimate source of power and authority is God Himself. God, the Father, has created the world and men in it, so that they might respond to Him in free, obedient love, thus becoming His sons and daughters. In so responding to His goodness and grace, men are also required to create and maintain among themselves personal and social relationships of the same quality as those which characterise the relationship each has with the Father. In other words, God's will is to be done not only in personal-individual terms, but also in the larger groupings and communities that characterise societies.

By his free choice, man has chosen to be disobedient and unbelieving – he has sinned against God, and endeavoured to erect an independent society and life centred around himself. From this primal disobedience come all the other divisions and separations which are the fabric of every individual life and all societies – man against himself, man against man, man against nature. The effects of this rebellion against God pervade all areas of human society, including institutions. Nothing has escaped the domination of sin. The forces of evil, personified in the being of Satan, have found access into the world through man's disobedience, and working through men have established a kingdom counter to that which the Father intends.

God sent Jesus Christ into the world to restore the relationship between Himself and man. Jesus Christ lived a life of perfect obedience to the Father. He was the one true human being Who exhibited in His daily life, in His words and works, what it means to do the Father's will. By His death on the cross, and resurrection from death He broke the power of Satan and sin over man, and made it possible for man to return to a life of fellowship with, and obedience to the Father. By faith in Christ's act, men are reconciled to God, freed from the dominion of darkness, and transferred to God's kingdom. Faith comes by the preaching, the hearing and the acting out of God's message of salvation in Jesus Christ.

Freed from this trap of his own and Satan's making, man is summoned to a life of obedience. The pattern for this life is Jesus Christ, and the power to live it is generated by Jesus Christ, who lives in the believer as the Holy Spirit. The Christian life, which begins in the individual, must extend outward into all areas of human society – into marriage and family relationships, into the fellowship of the church, into larger circles of every-day human relationships, and ultimately into all spheres of life: cultural, social, economic and political. There is no "pocket" or "zone" of human experience which is of *unconcern* to the Christian. He lives as the herald of God's good news in a still unbelieving world, witnessing to the message of salvation in both word and deed. In so living out this obedient life, the Christian confronts the entrenched power of sin and Satan which, though broken by Jesus Christ, still operates where men submit to its dominion. This results in conflict and struggle, usually experienced first in personal terms, and then in wider social and relational terms. The struggle is not only one of overcoming sin personally and socially, it is also one of building and restoring those personal and social conditions which will, in accordance with God's original and continuing intention, make it possible for men to live the "abundant life" which Jesus Himself promised.

One of the structures which God has provided for the benefit and well-being of His children is government, the so-called "political" realm. This is certainly the teaching of Romans 13. However, because government has also become the sphere of Satan's activity, the political realm is also one in which the Christian, as he lives his obedient life, may become engaged in struggle and conflict. It is precisely at those points where government (1) requires an obedience and loyalty that only God Himself can demand, (2) requires of the Christian a behaviour that is prohibited by Scripture or by the Spirit-informed Christian conscience, (3) ceases to function as the agent of God (Romans 13:6) and engages instead in brutal or unjust acts against its citizens (be they Christian or non-Christian), that the Christian is called upon to bear witness. The witness which he bears is that Jesus Christ is Lord of Lords, that only He can command total obedience. It is a warning that God Himself will judge governments and the human agents who wield political power by the way in which they exercise that power in the laws, policies and practices which they establish. And the Christian is compelled to do what he can, in accordance with the example and Spirit of Jesus Christ, not only to *point out* such evils, but also to *correct* them. He will speak truth to power. He will obey God rather than men. And he will submit to whatever penalty or punishment that may come as the result of his witness.

This is the political segment of life in which we have, by our actions, attempted to faithfully emulate our Lord's example.

There have been several specific criticisms levelled against us because of the kind of activity in which we have found ourselves involved. Although detailed and involved responses to these criticisms are obviously impossible in a letter of this nature, we nevertheless feel obligated to express to our fellow missionary colleagues our own feelings about the issues raised by them.

1 The first criticism is that as foreign missionaries we are guests in Korea and ought, therefore, to behave like guests. The inference here is, first, that engaging in "political activity" does not become the role of a guest, and secondly, that what we are doing is indeed political activity.

Aside from the fact that the presence of any foreigner in Korea today is in itself of deep political significance, we feel that this issue could be approached from a number of directions. Perhaps the simplest way to respond, however, would be to ask some relevant questions. How long, for example, must a missionary live in a foreign land before he ceases to be a guest? If a missionary chooses to identify himself as a guest, does this mean that the demands which the Lord places on him become secondary to those which the Korean government places upon him? What of Amos, who journeyed to a foreign land and spoke prophetically? And if we are really guests, who is the host? Is it the rulers of this nation or its people? Furthermore, what is the responsibility of the guest to his host? Does the guest sit quietly even if he discovers that his host has become ill or is dying? Why does a guest have the right to "meddle" in the most crucial aspect of life – the religious – but not the human?

Without wishing in any way to apply sarcasm to so grave an issue, we would look at the story of the Good Samaritan as an example of a foreigner who intervened in the affairs of others. Suppose the Good Samaritan had responded to the situation in which he found himself by saying, "I am a guest in your land and cannot get involved. You can be certain, however, that I will pray for you and also for those thieves who treated you so poorly."

2 A second criticism levelled against us is based on the Biblical injunction expressed in the 13th chapter of Paul's letter to the Romans, urging us to be subject to the governing authorities, for their authority is from God. Obviously in a letter of this sort we cannot hope to exhaust debate on this complex subject, but again a few comments seem in order. We wonder, for example, why this particular passage is singled out of all relevant Biblical texts on the subject. The Revelation of John, for example, written much later than Paul's Epistle and under a much more severe government, presents an effective diatribe against the ruling authorities and uses such expressions as "throne of the beast" in taking evil and corrupt rulers to task. The Old Testament abounds with instances of resistance to evil rulers: Moses in Egypt, Daniel and his friends, Samuel's rebukes of Saul when he got out of hand, to mention only a few. Why, then, among all the passages of the Bible concerning this issue, must we single out this particular one in the New Testament as our *ultimate* guide?

We wonder also how far those who uphold this particular passage of Scripture would go in adhering to it. Would they consistently apply it to every ruler who has ever existed or would they admit that there might be room for exceptions? Is it never wrong to serve an evil king? Does submission mean blind obedience? Is it not true that our ultimate obedience is always to God and that, although we ought to uphold our earthly rulers to the end of preserving order, we will ultimately find our allegiance to the Lord taking precedence? And is it not true also that those whose authority is from God, are in turn subject to God?

What do we do when the rulers in power have arrived there by forcibly overthrowing the previously existing powers, as is the case with our present government? Why were they not subservient to the previous rulers?

And finally, this statement must be applied to any nation which insists that it is still a democracy. In a democracy, the governing authorities are the people themselves and it is improper for any one person or group of persons to assume absolute power.

3 Issue number three deals with the theological understanding of the role of the missionary and finds the foreign missionary required to "limit himself to religious activity" or to "stick to preaching the gospel". Each person who raises this issue, be he missionary colleague or government official, has his own understanding of what that means. Basically, however, it is an attempt to radically dichotomise what are usually called "evangelism" and "social action". We regret the separation of these two because we find them to be common and inseparable concerns of Christ in the New Testament.

The Christian at Work Overseas

While calling men of all walks of life to a new birth, a new life and a new community, Christ healed the sick, fed the hungry and ministered to the poor, and at the same time directly challenged the authorities on such matters as working and healing on the sabbath. We frankly see no way to live in Korea as missionaries attempting to be true to Christ's example without sharing these concerns for the total life of man.

We are also bemused by an understanding of our role which seems to imply that the "religious" aspect of life is relatively unimportant and that, therefore, we can meddle in it as much as we please. One would think that those who insist on separating the "religious" from the "physical" or "earthly" would also insist that the religious is of most crucial importance. Nevertheless, we are offered free rein in this area even to the extent of government support of activities which it decides are genuinely religious.

This raises a challenging question: are we willing to let this or any other government determine what is or is not *proper religious activity?*

4 Another area of concern which has recently gained tremendous publicity and emphasis is the "national security" question. Many say that while freedom, justice and civil liberties are important, these must take second place to defence against the expansion of communism in Asia, and that therefore, those who are actively working for those issues must postpone their efforts in light of the more important priority of defence and security. We can only take this statement as a contradiction in terms. Without denying either the existence of the communist threat or its severity, we would make certain observations. We have recently observed the collapse of Vietnam, not because of lack of foreign aid in finances or man-power, but because the people of Vietnam were not sufficiently inspired by a succession of totalitarian leaders to resist aggression. We believe that Korea's greatest asset in countering communist aggression has long been the fierce anti-communist stance of the Korean people (and especially the Christians) based on a great desire for freedom and justice. By destroying freedom and justice, by trampling on human rights, by outlawing all voices of opposition or differing opinions, the Park regime is destroying the only hope of unity and common commitment to its goals, even to one as important as national security. The goals of national security are actually dependent upon an atmosphere and genuine support of democratic freedoms and justice but these are the very things which present government practices tend to smother. This in itself is, in our opinion, the real threat to national security.

5 The final criticism with which we will attempt to deal is what has quite properly been called "don't stick our neck out". Actions by some missionaries which upset the government result in inconveniences for all missionaries who suddenly find that they are under surveillance and that it is more difficult than previously to obtain visas, residence permits and tax exemptions. This is perhaps the most difficult of all the criticisms to answer because we are sensitive to what is happening and we do feel badly that our involvement has caused inconvenience to others.

But let us place the issue in the most glaring light possible. Through exhaustive research, prayer and personal involvement based on our own understanding of Jesus's words in Matthew 25:31 ff, we came to feel that eight essentially innocent men were executed by the Korean government. Can we honourably remain quiet in such a situation? In other words, which is ultimately more important, innocent death or inconvenience?

And finally, we would beg your understanding as we turn this issue around and point out that others' actions and involvement affect us also. Those who support this government either directly or through indifference and silence, make it extremely difficult not only for us, but even more important, for the millions of Korean citizens who long for a just and humane life.

We hope that this letter will foster a greater understanding and co-operation in the Lord's work. We hope that you will accept it in a spirit of love, knowing that it is not meant to be a closed or final statement, but that we offer it as an open ended statement, realising our need for continuing growth, new insights and open dialogue with all our brothers and sisters in Christ. The Spirit gives each of us a special and different function in His service, and yet we believe that out of this diversity we are, each one, working to build up the Body of Christ which is the Church.

If you are interested in getting together for a more personal dialogue, either for further exploration or clarification, please contact us.

W Ransom Rice Jr.	Marion Current
Suzanne Rice	Ian Robb
Basil M Price	Jo-anne Fisher
Robert J Kelly	Delores Smiskol
Sean Dwan	Madeleine Guisto
Gene Matthews	Richard Petersen
William A Basinger	Didier t'Serstevens
Charles A Krauth	Dorothea Schweizer
Fran Krauth	Harriet P Moon
Walter F Durst	Jack Corcoran
Louise M Durst	Benedict Zweber
Willa Kernen	Pat Ryan

Fellowship with the Home Church

An article by The Rev Patrick Goodland

Among a variety of penetrating analogies concerning the nature of the Church, the New Testament uses the idea of an ideal family. This is both relevant and important to the theme under consideration.

As Christians we can never be unduly individualistic. Any enterprise in which we have a part and which is seeking to fulfil our Lord's teaching is in measure a reflection of the work of the body – 1 Cor. 12. It is essential before we seek, in Christ's name, to help the homeless or nurse the victims of some disaster that we are a part of the brotherhood – 1 Peter 2:17. It is spoken of as "the household of faith" – Gal. 6:10 and in Eph. 2:19 – "the household of God". We rejoice together in the truth of Rev. 5:9 and are to experiment with this fact in service.

The ideal is not often the reality, but where a fellowship/church see their representative, team worker, international Christian worker, or the training college student as an extension of their own local work, there can be deep mutual strengthening.

The fellowship links need to be stimulated. In a cardiac arrest it is sometimes necessary to inject stimulants. Sometimes our church body needs to be informed concerning our part in an enterprise that they may be able to share.

Some suggested stimulants!

Before you leave for service

1 At an early stage share with your minister or oversight something of your concern and your proposed course of action.

2 Seek opportunities through your church leaders to share with the church body and its constituent organisations. Distribute relevant TEAR Fund/mission literature to interested groups and arrange for a supply to be sent during your absence.

3 To share you will need information. Read about the country, its habits, customs, religions and its culture, and be clear in your mind as far as possible, what it is you are hoping to do.

4 A limited number of members may be prepared to give time for prayer while you are overseas. Cultivate their interest. You will find time spent in encouraging a prayer cell will be very profitable when you are isolated from the familiar and living in the unfamiliar.

While you are away on service

TEAR Fund and the societies are interested in 'wholeness' for people in New Testament terms in the areas in which they engage in work. Charity/relief work which is devoid of faith and hope is bankrupt. Bread for the body is not enough, they must have it with hope. If home fellowship is to be encouraged, our work assisted and our personal integrity and spiritual life kept at an abundant level we shall need to communicate regularly.

One of the dangers of a busy life is the breakdown of communication. This can be disturbing to the family and detrimental to the individual. We are members of a body and our spiritual life is in measure in dependence on others. People cannot have an intelligent prayer life without information.

1 Time spent in correspondence needs to be scheduled in your weekly agenda. Inevitably much of our work among destitute, needy people is exhausting and physically demanding. We must be careful that we do not isolate ourselves – a card a week will assure you of maintained interest at home. I have met numerous overseas workers who have suffered psychological disorders through feelings of loneliness and isolation because they have not had the privilege of 'body' backing.

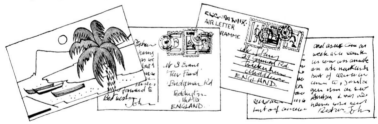

2 Tell it as it is! – a slogan adopted some years ago by some missions. Joy and sorrows, encouragements and difficulties, triumphs and defeats should be shared – Rom. 12:15. Your humanness makes you real to your church family. Let them see situations through your eyes – this can challenge and provoke the complacency of much western Christianity and lead to deeper identification with God's 'other sheep' – 2 Tim. 1:7–9.

3 In identification with suffering humanity, homeless people and the results of the depravity of human cruelty, there is sometimes a tendency to be impatient with the home church. If you are young, rebellious attitudes may begin to flare in your mind – 'why haven't the older members of the body done something about this before?' Careful before you criticise – many at home would love to have the opportunity to actually minister with *their* hands and *their* head, but there was little knowledge and opportunity when they were younger.

When you return from service

Homecoming can produce powerful emotions. I well remember the nausea and near anger which boiled up inside of me on seeing people waste food in England after our mission to the pathetic famine victims in Ethiopia. Pray for the grace of control, patience and the opportunity to educate to a better way.

1 The culture shock in reverse is not uncommon. Share your feelings and resentments with your minister or trusted elders. Allow the body to minister to you. Jesus sent out His disciples two by two because He knew that the joys of success or the sorrows of disappointment can easily lead either to pride or depression. This is where the body can minister.

2 Let the privilege of service remind us of our continuing responsibility to the world's needy. Share your experiences with your church.

3 Living in the west with communications, transport and adequate supplies, it is very easy to reflect on the inadequacies of those who are at the front of the fight. In retrospect you may feel that the organisation or permanent personnel could be more efficient. There may be much truth in your reasoning. Often the front line troops have been battling to the point of exhaustion. Invariably their inadequacies are dictated by their circumstances, shortages of finance and personnel. We need, therefore, to be lenient and discreet in any public criticism of their shortcomings.

We want to support you – How can we do this?

Some practical hints from the Editor to share with others

Please consider sending me regularly –

my church magazine
a monthly cassette tape with my home church's services
a Christian monthly magazine
    e.g. 'Today', 130 City Road, London, EC1V 2NJ
        'Buzz', 51 Haydons Road, London SW19 1HG
        'Family', 51 Haydons Road, London SW19 1HG
        'Third Way', 130 City Road, London EC1V 2NJ
a weekly news magazine
    e.g. Time-Life International B.V., Ottho Heldringstraat 5, Amsterdam 1018, Holland
OR a weekly national newspaper
    e.g. The Guardian Weekly – 164 Deansgate, Manchester, M60 2RR

N.B.: Most newspapers/magazines can be sent at a special cheap airmail rate if packed properly – details from the Post Office.

The Christian at Work Overseas

Please consider sending me from time to time —

Christian and secular music cassettes
Bible-reading cassettes
Christian and secular books/paperbacks
Occasional food parcels
Photographs of family, friends and Christian fellowship activities
Technical Information in relation to my profession
    e.g. relevant professional magazine
          Intermediate Technology magazine — 9 King Street, London, WC2E 8HN

N.B.:   Before having items sent out, it would be important to discover the details
        concerning customs regulations and payments of duties.

Please consider receiving —

my circular prayer letter every 3/4 months
the regular materials/magazine from my sponsoring body

Please consider arranging or joining —

a prayer group for my area of work overseas
a special evening focusing on my work (if planned well in advance, I will send back a
cassette, slides and menu ideas)

Please consider giving —

towards my personal support on a regular basis
towards the general needs of my area of work

(N.B.: Different missions/societies have varying policies concerning finance).

Thank You!

Culture Shock in Reverse

Some thoughts on problems faced by workers returning from overseas

Forgive the rather terrifying title! These are merely notes resulting from individual meetings and one or two seminars with those recently returned from working overseas under Tear Fund's Short Term Overseas Personnel programme. Many people have found it comparatively easy to settle back into the different culture and environment of the United Kingdom after their period of two or three years' service abroad, but for others the journey from Dacca, Nairobi, or San Jose has brought with it very real difficulties – and it is important for us all to be aware of the problems involved, both for ourselves and for those we meet under these sorts of pressures.

For many of those reading this while overseas, there will be growing excitement at the prospect of returning home in the next few weeks or months – and, as thoughts increasingly turn to cornflakes, cricket and the Cotswolds, the temptation is to build up a picture of a quiet, settled, secure homeland with none of the problems of loneliness, language limitations and harsh living conditions of the last couple of years. This is because, if one word is to sum up the situation you will find on returning home, that word is CHANGE – and it is the change in conditions, in surroundings and in relationships which lies at the root of all culture shock. In fact many overseas workers have found the strains and tensions on their return to the United Kingdom every bit as hard as those encountered two or three years earlier in the initial months abroad.

Change in Christian Friends

There will be change in Christian friends and perhaps even one's immediate family. Some may be married, with new priorities on their time; others will have moved to new areas. All will have changed and after seeing harsh living conditions in other areas of the world, their lifestyle may seem permeated with materialism, caught up with the apparent trivialities of the local situation, and blind to issues and tensions beyond the immediate environment.

Change in the home church

The close prayerful fellowship of the Christian team overseas often contrasts quite sharply with the rather superficial concern and interest of some local churches in this country. A lack of meaningful relationships within the body and a distorted idea of Christian work abroad tends to place the recently returned "missionary" on a spiritual pedestal, with the constant pressure of having to live up to the expectations of others – or, at the other extreme, the short-termer may be expected to slot back normally into church activities as if the last couple of years have merely been an "interesting holiday". Prayer groups wanting to hear success stories rather than the often depressing, uncomfortable realities; little appreciation by Christian friends of their material benefits; a distressingly wasteful use of money; complacency; little relevance to, concern for, or impact on an increasingly degenerate society – it may be all too apparent to the new arrival. Even the hard-pressed staff of the sponsoring missionary society can seem too busy to have as deep an interest as they would like in any not offering for a further spell overseas.

Change in society

Walk into the supermarket – 27 different types of breakfast cereals on the shelves. Look outside, to see the constant endless rush of traffic... people with grim faces hastening to their next appointment. Then think back three days to Bangladesh or Nigeria – a mother unable to beg enough food for her malnourished child, the farmers labouring on arid ground with medieval tools. It isn't fair – and, however much British society may or may not have changed over the last two years, the worker returning from overseas inevitably feels out of touch, a self-conscious country cousin.

However trivial style of dress may seem in an African village, in Britain fashions have been changing constantly. Your whole wardrobe is dated – and you may feel you have to keep in touch with fashion, if only to avoid the standard image of the missionary on furlough. But clothing's not the only problem, and finances are not likely to be too healthy either. Humour, language, interests, tastes, lifestyle – these too will have changed in the last couple of years. Even standards acceptable in one's own Christian circle may be significantly different now and certainly will stand in direct contrast to the attitudes of many national Christians overseas.

Change in yourself

The greatest change for most people after a term of service overseas will be in themselves. The tremendously valuable experience of living, working and witnessing in a strange culture must challenge many of the ideas, beliefs and priorities previously taken for granted. The return to the UK can bring bewilderment, insecurity, frustration and anger ... *or* the new experiences can be channelled positively, even prophetically, to enrich and contribute to the awareness, involvement and commitment of church and society at home.

There is change brought on by the attitudes and expectations of those around – the pressures of altered relationships, of the "missionary image", of recounting untiringly the same descriptions and stories, and the fear of drawing attention to self when only too aware of one's own pathetically insignificant contribution to the Lord's work. And from within there may be the feeling of guilt. Guilt brought on by anger and inward criticism of the superficiality of fellowship and part-time Christianity. Guilt perhaps at seemingly accomplishing so little while overseas and now at one's own diminishing concern for the on-going work. Frustration at the inability to communicate meaningfully. All intensified by inevitable physical tiredness, a natural temptation towards self-pity, and often an uncertainty over what the future holds in store.

Any answers?

There can be a tendency to dramatise and exaggerate these culture shock problems. We are all surprisingly resilient and adaptable and many people, as we have seen, are able to slip naturally back into society, enriched by their experiences and using their new understanding to contribute to life around. Others however, returning perhaps from other countries or to more difficult environments, have found in different measure that these changes in relationships and surroundings can for a while cause considerable upsets and unhappiness.

Here we can only pass on one or two basic tips which others have found helpful.

Keep in touch with God

Often underlying the insecurity and uncertainty are spiritual tensions – for some a bewilderment and anger with the Lord and fellow believers, for others a temporary spiritual collapse away from the fellowship of the missionary team. This may just be a result of tiredness and lack of privacy – i.e. have a good get-away-from-it-all-holiday! – but it is clearly important also from the beginning to look for a pastor who will appreciate the problems involved. Then the Lord can use you where He's put you now ...

Keep in touch with home

The obvious way of reducing the impact of the overseas/UK contrast is to keep fully abreast of news (and gossip!) from home while still abroad. Not only does this allow a more informed prayerful concern and prevent too intense a preoccupation with the immediate situation, but it means that one returns aware that pork chops have doubled in price and that stiletto heels are definitely out for this year! Get local papers, magazines and current price lists sent out.

Realise that unemployment is now a major worry in the UK, even for trained personnel, and be prepared for a hard slog to find a suitable job. Communication however is a two-way process, and, if friends and the church are to support intelligently and to help constructively on your return, it is important that they are kept regularly and honestly informed of the work and conditions overseas – otherwise there is only one person to blame when, returning from Nigeria, you are asked how you got on in the deserts of Bangladesh ... Some people have found it helpful to stop off once or twice on the journey home, giving the chance of a good rest before returning home and allowing a more gradual acclimatisation to Western culture.

Keep in touch with the future

The temptation is to think that, even if the world does not stop when you arrive back in Hereford, at least there is time for a well-earned break before making any plans for the future. With the current unemployment difficulties, however, and the need to update one's training, this can (and sometimes has) led to several months of drifting and the inevitable danger of boredom, frustration and uncertainty. Some short-term workers, of course, come back to the UK planning to return overseas in the near future. Others start courses for further qualifications or at Bible College. Others will be getting married. Many, on the other hand, have not really looked beyond the present or seriously asked the Lord where He is leading them on to – it is important while still overseas to be thinking and praying ahead. Supporting churches and fellowships can be encouraged to enquire about refresher courses or Bible training, or to keep an eye open for suitable employment possibilities.

Keep in touch with missionary colleagues

Many find it helpful to keep in contact with the missionary society and with former colleagues also now back in this country. In fact even when 8,000 miles from your overseas work, there are still ways to continue serving the programme there – through encouragement, prayer, raising support (bring good slides back) and acting on their behalf in the UK. The short-term workers still overseas will be helped by hearing your impressions and reactions on returning home – and they can help you by reminding you of the realities of their on-going work.

Finally

Praise God for the variety of His creation, enjoy what is good in Western society, criticise what is wrong, and remember that ...

"we are His workmanship, created in Christ Jesus for good works, which God prepared beforehand, that we should walk in them." (Ephesians 2:10)

PART TWO:

Theological

Mission

by the Rev John Stott
(an extract from 'Christian Mission in the Modern World' published by Falcon)

The first word we have to consider is 'mission'. Before attempting a Biblical definition it may be helpful to take a look at the contemporary polarization.

Two Extreme Views

The older or traditional view has been to equate mission and evangelism, missionaries and evangelists, missions and evangelistic programmes. Even the Commission on World Mission and Evangelism did not distinguish in its constitution between 'mission' and 'evangelism', but defined its aim as 'to further the proclamation to the whole world of the gospel of Jesus Christ, to the end that all men may believe in Him and be saved'. As Philip Potter said in his address to the WCC Central Committee, meeting in Crete in 1967, 'ecumenical literature since Amsterdam has used "mission", "witness" and "evangelism" interchangeably.

In its extreme form this older view of mission as consisting exclusively of evangelism also concentrated on verbal proclamation. The missionary was often caricatured as standing under a palm tree, wearing a sola topi, and declaiming the gospel to a group of ill-clad natives sitting respectfully round him on the ground. Thus the traditional image of the missionary was of the preacher, and a rather paternalistic kind of preacher at that. Such an emphasis on the priority of evangelistic preaching left little room in some cases even for the founding of Christian schools. Philip Crowe told us at the 1968 Islington Conference of a certain R.N. Cust who argued in 1888 that missionary money 'was collected for the purpose of converting a soul, not sharpening an intellect'. He slightly modified his position in 1894 to include 'a lay evangelist, a female evangelist, a medical evangelist whenever gospel preaching is the substantive work', but added: 'when it is proposed to have a pious industrial superintendent, or an evangelical tile manufacturer, or a low church breeder of cattle or raiser of turnips, I draw my line' ('Mission in the Modern World', Patmos 1968).

This is a very extreme example, however. Most adherents of the traditional view of mission would regard education and medical work as perfectly proper, and indeed as very useful adjuncts to evangelistic work, often out of Christian compassion for the ignorant and the sick, though sometimes as being unashamedly 'platforms' or 'springboards' for evangelism — hospitals and schools providing in their patients and pupils a conveniently captive audience for the gospel. In either case the mission itself was understood in terms of evangelism.

This traditional view is far from being dead and buried. The so-called 'Jesus movement' has encouraged the formation of Christian communes into which zealous young evangelicals withdraw from the wicked world. For a commune easily degenerates into a compound, and even into a quasi-monastic establishment. Then the only contact which such Christians have with the world (which they regard as totally and irredeemably wicked) is to make occasional evangelistic raids into it. Apocalyptic imagery comes natural to them. The world is like a building on fire, they say; a Christian's only duty is to mount a rescue operation before it is too late. Jesus Christ is coming at any moment; there is no point in tampering with the structures of society, for society is doomed and about to be destroyed. Besides, any attempt to improve society is bound to be unproductive since unrenewed men cannot build a new world. Man's only hope lies in being born again. Only then might society conceivably be reborn. But it is too late now even for that.

Such world-denying pessimism is a strange phenomenon in those who say they believe in God. But then their image of God is only partially shaped by the Biblical revelation. He is not the Creator who in the beginning gave man a 'cultural mandate' to subdue and rule the earth, who has instituted governing authorities as His 'ministers' to order society and maintain justice, and who, as the Lausanne Covenant puts it, because He is 'both the Creator and the Judge of all men' is concerned for 'justice and reconciliation throughout human society' (para 5).

At the opposite extreme to this unBiblical concept of mission as consisting of evangelism alone there is the standard ecumenical viewpoint, at least since the middle 1960s and the preparatory work for the Uppsala Assembly. The publication in 1967 of the reports of the West European and North American working groups on 'the missionary structure of the congregation', entitled 'The Church for Others' (WCC), gave currency to a whole new vocabulary of mission. The thesis developed in these reports was that God is at work in the historical process, that the purpose of his mission, of the *missio Dei*, is the establishment of *shalom* (Hebrew for 'peace') in the sense of social harmony, and that this *shalom* (which it was suggested is identical with the kingdom of God) is exemplified in 'the emancipation of coloured races, the concern for the humanization of industrial relations, various attempts at rural development, the quest for business and professional ethics, the concern for intellectual honesty and integrity' ('The Church for Others', p 15).

Moreover, in working towards this goal God uses 'men and women both inside and outside the churches', and the church's particular role in the mission of God is to 'point to God at work in world history' (p 16), to discover what He is doing, to catch up with it and to get involved in it ourselves. For God's primary relationship is to the world, it was argued, so that the true sequence is to be found no longer in the formula 'God-church-world' but in the formula 'God-world-church' (p 16). This being so, 'it is the world that must be allowed to provide the agenda for the churches' (p 20). — the churches taking the world seriously and seeking to serve according to its contemporary sociological needs.

Professor J.G. Davies, who had been a member of the West European working group, expressed similar ideas in his two books 'Worship and Mission' (SCM 1966) and 'Dialogue with the World' (SCM 1967). He equated humanization, reconciliation, *shalom* and the setting up of God's kingdom as being together the goal of mission ('Dialogue' pp 12—16). 'Hence mission is concerned with the overcoming of industrial disputes, with the surmounting of class divisions, with the eradication of racial discrimination' (p 14). Indeed, 'We are required to enter into partnership with God in history to renew society' (p 15).

Much of this attempted reconstruction of 'mission' was quoted in the 'Drafts for Sections', which were published in preparation for Uppsala. Mission was seen as the historical process of the renewal of society, and the theme text of Uppsala was 'Behold, I make all things new' (Revelation 21:5). But this word of God is an eschatological affirmation. It is uttered from the throne (in John's vision), almost immediately after the new heaven and the new earth have appeared. Yet several times at Uppsala it was used as an expression not of future hope but of present reality, not of the final regeneration of the universe but of 'the acceleration of social and political change'.

Apart from this misuse of Scripture, what are we to say about the identification of the mission of God with social renewal? A fourfold critique may be made. First, the God who is Lord of history is also the Judge of history. It is naïve to hail all revolutionary movements as signs of divine renewal. After the revolution the new status quo sometimes enshrines more injustice and oppression than the one it has displaced.

Secondly, the Biblical categories of *shalom*, the new humanity and the kingdom of God are not to be identified with social renewal. It is true that in the Old Testament *shalom* (peace) often indicates political and material well-being. But can it be maintained, as serious Biblical exegesis, that the New Testament authors present Jesus Christ as winning this kind of peace and as bestowing it on society as a whole? To assume that all Old Testament prophecies are fulfilled in literal and material terms is to make the very mistake which Jesus' contemporaries made when they tried to take Him by force and make Him a king (John 5:15). The New Testament understanding of Old Testament prophecy is that its fulfilment transcends the categories in which the promises were given. So according to the apostles the peace which Jesus preaches and gives is something deeper and richer, namely reconciliation and fellowship with God and with each other (eg Ephesians 2:13-22). Moreover, He does not bestow it on all men but on those who belong to Him, to His redeemed community. So *shalom* is the blessing the Messiah brings to His people. The new creation and the new humanity are to be seen in those who are in Christ (2 Corinthians 5:17); and the kingdom has to be received like a little child (Mark 10:15). Certainly it is our Christian duty to commend by argument and example the righteous standards of the kingdom to those who have not themselves received or entered it. In this way we see the righteousness of the kingdom, as it were, 'spilling over' into segments of the world and thus to some extent blurring the frontiers between the two. Nevertheless the kingdom remains distinct from godless society, and actually entry into it depends on spiritual rebirth.

Thirdly, the word 'mission' cannot properly be used to cover everything God is doing in the world. In providence and common grace He is indeed active in all men and all societies, whether they acknowledge Him or not. But this is not His 'mission'. 'Mission' concerns His redeemed people, and what He sends them into the world to do.

Fourthly, Uppsala's preoccupation with social change left little or no room for evangelistic concern. It was this imbalance against which, if I may speak personally, I felt I had to protest at the plenary session at which the report of Section II 'Renewal in Mission' was made.

'The Assembly has given its earnest attention to the hunger, poverty and injustices of the contemporary world', I said. 'Rightly so. I have myself been moved by it. But I do not find a comparable concern or compassion for the spiritual hunger of men ... The church's first priority ... remains the millions and millions ... who (as Christ and His apostles tell us again and again) being without Christ are perishing ... The World Council of Churches professes to acknowledge Jesus Christ as Lord. Well, the Lord Jesus Christ sent His church to preach the good news and make disciples; I do not see this Assembly as a whole eager to obey His command. The Lord Jesus Christ wept over the impenitent city which had rejected Him; I do not see this Assembly weeping any similar tears.

A Biblical Synthesis?

From the traditional view of mission as exclusively evangelistic and the current ecumenical view of it as the establishment of *shalom*, we ask if there is a better way, a more balanced and more Biblical way of defining the mission of the church, and of relating to one another the evangelistic and social responsibilities of the people of God. The delegates to the meeting of the Commission on World Mission and Evangelism in Mexico City in December 1963 saw the problem, but said they were unable to find a solution. They confessed in the report of Section III:

'Debate returned again and again to the relationship between God's action in and through the Church and everything God is doing in the world apparently independently of the Christian community. Can a distinction be drawn between God's providential action and God's redeeming action? ... We were able to state thesis and antithesis in this debate, but we could not see our way through to the truth which we feel lies beyond this dialectic'. ('Witness in Six Continents' edited by R K Orchard, Edinburgh House Press 1964 p 157).

Many came to Uppsala hoping for a genuine meeting of minds by which this tension could be resolved. In one of the opening speeches Dr W A Visser t'Hooft expressed the hope that the Assembly would deal with this issue 'positively and ecumenically' – 'positively in the sense that we give a clear sense of orientation to our movement' and 'ecumenically in the sense that we will truly listen to each other'. He went on to make his own contribution by saying:

'I believe that, with regard to the great tension between the vertical interpretation of the Gospel as essentially concerned with God's saving action in the life of individuals, and the horizontal interpretation of it as mainly concerned with human relationships in the world, we must get out of that rather primitive oscillating movement of going from one extreme to the other, which is not worthy of a movement which by its nature seeks to embrace the truth of the gospel in its fulness. A Christianity which has lost its vertical dimension has lost its salt and is not only insipid in itself, but useless for the world. But a Christianity which would use the vertical preoccupation as a means to escape from its responsibility for and in the common life of man is a denial of the incarnation, of God's love for the world manifested in Christ' ('The Uppsala 68 Report' edited by Norman Goodall, WCC, Geneva 1968 pp 317-18).

But unfortunately what Mexico left unfinished Uppsala did not complete, and Dr Visser t'Hooft's hope was unfulfilled. The old polarization continues.

All of us should be able to agree that mission arises primarily out of the nature not of the church but of God Himself. The living God of the Bible is a sending God. I think it was Johannes Blauw in his book 'The Missionary Nature of the Church' (McGraw-Hill 1962) who first used the word 'centrifugal' to describe the church's mission. Then Professor J G Davies applied it to God Himself. God, he writes is 'a centrifugal Being'. ('Worship and Mission', 1966, p 28). It is a dramatic figure of speech. Yet it is only another way of saying that God is love, always reaching out after others in self-giving service.

So he sent forth Abraham, commanding him to go from his country and kindred into the great unknown, and promising to bless him and to bless the world through him if he obeyed (Genesis 12:1-3). Next, He sent Joseph into Egypt, overruling even his brothers' cruelty, in order to preserve a godly remnant on earth during the famine (Genesis 45:4-8). Then He sent Moses to His oppressed people in Egypt, with good news of liberation, saying to him: 'Come, I will send you to Pharoah that you may bring forth my people ... out of Egypt' (Exodus 3:10). After the Exodus and the settlement He sent a continuous succession of prophets with words of warning and of promise to His people.

As He said through Jeremiah: 'From the day that your fathers came out of the land of Egypt to this day, I have persistently sent all my servants the prophets to them, day after day, yet they did not listen to me ...' (Jeremiah 7:25, 26 cf Chronicles 36:15,16).
After the Babylonian captivity He graciously sent them back to the land, and sent more messengers with them and to them to help them rebuild the temple, the city and the national life. Then at last 'when the time had fully come, God sent forth His Son'; and after that the Father and the Son sent forth the Spirit on the Day of Pentecost (Galatians 4:4-6; John 14:26; 15:26; 16:7; Acts 2:33).

All this is the essential Biblical background to any understanding of mission. The primal mission is God's, for it is He who sent His prophets, His Son, His Spirit. Of these missions the mission of the Son is central, for it was the culmination of the ministry of the prophets, and it embraced within itself as its climax the sending of the Spirit. And now the Son sends as He Himself was sent. Already during His public ministry He sent out first the apostles and then the seventy as a kind of extension of His own preaching, teaching and healing ministry. Then after His death and resurrection He widened the scope of the mission to include all who call Him Lord and themselves His disciples. For others were present with the twelve when the Great Commission was given (eg Luke 24:33). We cannot restrict its application to the apostles.

The Great Commission

This brings us to a consideration of the terms of the Great Commission. What was it that the Lord Jesus commissioned His people to do? There can be no doubt that most versions of it (for He seems to have repeated it in several forms on several occasions) place the emphasis on evangelism. 'Go into all the world and preach the gospel to the whole creation' is the familiar command of the 'longer ending' of Mark's gospel which seems to have been added by some later hand after Mark's original conclusion was lost (Mark 16:15). 'Go ... and make disciples of all nations, baptising them ... and teaching them ...' is the Matthean form (Matthew 28:19,20), while Luke records at the end of his gospel Christ's word 'that repentance and forgiveness of sins should be preached in His name to all nations' and at the beginning of the Acts that His people would receive power to become His witnesses to the end of the earth (Luke 24:47; Acts 1:8). The cumulative emphasis seems clear. It is placed on preaching, witnessing and making disciples, and many deduce from this that the mission of the church, according to the specification of the risen Lord, is exclusively a preaching, converting and teaching mission. Indeed, I confess that I myself argued this at the World Congress on Evangelism in Berlin in 1966, when attempting to expound the three major versions of the Great Commission.

Today, however, I would express myself differently. It is not just that the commission includes a duty to teach converts everything Jesus had previously commanded (Matthew 28:20), and that social responsibility is among the things which Jesus commanded. I now see more clearly that not only the consequences of the commission but the actual commission itself must be understood to include social as well as evangelistic responsibility, unless we are to be guilty of distorting the words of Jesus.

The crucial form in which the Great Commission has been handed down to us (though it is the most neglected because it is the most costly) is the Johannine. Jesus had anticipated it in His prayer in the upper room when He said to the Father: 'As thou didst send me into the world, so I have sent them into the world' (John 17:18). Now, probably in the same upper room but after His death and resurrection, He turned His prayer-statement into a commission and said: 'As the Father has sent Me, even so I send you' (John 20:21). In both these sentences Jesus did more than draw a vague parallel between His mission and ours. Deliberately and precisely He made His mission the model of ours, saying 'as the Father sent me, so I send you'. Therefore our understanding of the Church's mission must be deduced from our understanding of the Son's. Why and how did the Father send the Son?

Of course the major purpose of the Son's coming into the world was unique. Perhaps it is partly for this reason that Christians have been hesitant to think of their mission as in any sense comparable to His. For the Father sent the Son to be the Saviour of the world, and to that end to atone for our sins and to bring us eternal life (1 John 4:9,10,14). Indeed, He Himself said He had come 'to seek and to save the lost' (Luke 19:10). We cannot copy Him in these things. We are not saviours. Nevertheless, all this is still an inadequate statement of why He came.

It is better to begin with something more general and say that He came to serve. His contemporaries were familiar with Daniel's apocalyptic vision of the son of man receiving dominion and being served by all peoples (Daniel 7:14). But Jesus knew He had to serve before He would be served, and to endure suffering before He would receive dominion. So He fused two apparently incompatible Old Testament images, Daniel's son of man and Isaiah's suffering servant, and said: 'the Son of man ... came not to be served but to serve, and to give His life a ransom for many' (Mark 10:45). The ransoming sin-offering was a sacrifice which He alone could offer, but this was to be the climax of a life of service, and we too may serve. 'I am among you' He said on another occasion 'as one who serves' (Luke 22:27). So He gave Himself in selfless service for others, and His service took a wide variety of forms according to men's needs. Certainly He preached, proclaiming the good news of the kingdom of God and teaching about the coming and the nature of the kingdom, how to enter it and how it would spread. But He served in deed as well as in word, and it would be impossible in the ministry of Jesus to separate His works from His words. He fed hungry mouths and washed dirty feet, He healed the sick, comforted the sad and even restored the dead to life.

Now He sends us, He says, as the Father had sent Him. Therefore our mission, like His, is to be one of service. He emptied Himself of status and took the form of a servant, and His humble mind is to be in us (Philippians 2:5-8). He supplies us with the perfect model of service, and sends His church into the world to be a servant church. Is it not essential for us to recover this Biblical emphasis? In many of our Christian attitudes and enterprises we have tended (especially those of us who live in Europe and North America) to be rather bosses than servants. Yet it seems that it is in our servant role that we can find the right synthesis of evangelism and social action. For both should be for us, as they undoubtedly were for Christ, authentic expressions of the love that serves.

Then there is another aspect of the mission of the Son which is to be paralleled in the mission of the church, namely that in order to serve He was sent into the world. He did not touch down like a visitor from outer space, or arrive like an alien bringing His own alien culture with Him. He took to Himself our humanity, our flesh and blood, our culture. He actually became one of us and experienced our frailty, our suffering and our temptations. He even bore our sin and died our death. And now He sends us 'into the world', to identify with others as He identified with us (though without losing our Christian identity), to become vulnerable as He did. It is surely one of the most characteristic failures of us Christians, not least of us who are called evangelical Christians, that we seldom seem to take seriously this principle of the Incarnation. 'As our Lord took on our flesh', runs the report from Mexico City 1963, 'so He calls His Church to take on the secular world. This is easy to say and sacrificial to do' ('Witness in Six Continents' p 151). It comes more natural to us to shout the gospel at people from a distance than to involve ourselves deeply in their lives, to think ourselves into their culture and their problems, and to feel with them in their pains. Yet this implication of our Lord's example is inescapable. As the Lausanne Covenant put it: 'We affirm that Christ sends His redeemed people into the world as the Father sent Him, and that this calls for a similar deep and costly penetration of the world' (para 6).

The Relation between Evangelism and Social Action

What, then should be the relation between evangelism and social action within our total Christian responsibility? If we grant that we have no liberty either to concentrate on evangelism to the exclusion of social concern or to make social activism a substitute for evangelism, we still need to define the relation between the two. Three main ways of doing this have been attempted.

First, some regard social action as a means to evangelism. In this case evangelism and the winning of converts are the primary ends in view, but social action is a useful preliminary, an effective means to these ends. In its most blatant form this makes social work (whether food, medicine or education) the sugar on the pill, the bait on the hook, while in its best form it gives to the gospel a credibility it would otherwise lack. In either case the smell of hypocrisy hangs round our philanthropy. A frankly ulterior motive impels us to engage in it. And the result of making our social programme the means to another end is that we breed so-called 'rice Christians'. This is inevitable if we ourselves have been 'rice evangelists'. They caught the deception from us. No wonder Gandhi said in 1931: 'I hold that proselytizing under the cloak of humanitarian work is, to say the least, unhealthy ... why should I change my religion because a doctor who professes Christianity as his religion has cured me of some disease ...?'

The second way of relating evangelism and social action is better. It regards social action not as a means to evangelism but as a manifestation of evangelism, or at least of the gospel which is being proclaimed. In this case philanthropy is not attached to evangelism rather artificially from the outside, but grows out of it as its natural expression. One might almost say that social action becomes the 'sacrament' of evangelism, for it makes the message significantly visible. J Herman Bavinck in his famous book 'An Introduction to the Science of Missions' (published 1954 in Holland, and 1960 by the Presbyterian and Reformed Publishing Co) defends this view. Medicine and education are more than 'a legitimate and necessary means of creating an opportunity for preaching', he writes, for 'if these services are motivated by the proper love and compassion, then they cease to be simply preparation, and at that very moment become preaching' (p 113). We should not hesitate to agree with this, so far as it goes, for there is a strong precedent for it in the ministry of Jesus. His words and deeds belonged to each other, the words interpreting the deeds and the deeds embodying the words. He did not only announce the good news of the kingdom; He performed visible 'signs of the kingdom'. If people would not believe His words, He said, then let them believe Him 'for the sake of the words themselves' (John 14:11).

Bishop John V Taylor takes a somewhat similar line in his contribution to the 'Christian Foundations' series entitled 'For All the World' (Hodder and Stoughton 1966). He writes of a 'three-stranded presentation of the Gospel' (p 43), by which he means that Christians are called to 'articulate the gospel ... through what they say (proclamation), what they are (witness) and what they do (service)' (p 40). This also is true, and finely said. Yet it leaves me uneasy. For it makes service a subdivision of evangelism, an aspect of the proclamation. I do not deny that good works of love did have an evidential value when performed by Jesus and do have an evidential value when performed by us (cf Matthew 5:16). But I cannot bring myself to accept that this is their only or even major justification. If it is, then still, and rather self-consciously at that, they are only a means to an end. If good works are visible preaching, then they are expecting a return; but if good works are visible loving, then they are 'expecting nothing in return' (Luke 6:35).

This brings me to the third way of stating the relation between evangelism and social action, which I believe to be the truly Christian one, namely that social action is a partner of evangelism. As partners the two belong to each other and yet are independent of each other. Each stands on its own feet in its own right alongside the other. Neither is a means to the other, or even a manifestation of the other. For each is an end in itself. Both are expressions of unfeigned love. As the National Evangelical Anglican Congress at Keele put it in 1967 'Evangelism and compassionate service belong together in the mission of God' (para 2:20).

The apostle John has helped me to grasp this by these words from his first letter: 'If anyone has the world's goods and sees his brother in need, yet closes his heart against him, how does God's love abide in him? Little children, let us not love in word or speech but in deed and in truth' (1 John 3:17,18). Here love in action springs from a twofold situation, first 'seeing' a brother in need and secondly 'having' the wherewithal to meet the need. If I do not relate what I 'have' to what I 'see', I cannot claim to be indwelt by the love of God. Further, this principle applies whatever the nature of the seen need. I may see spiritual need (sin, guilt, lostness) and have the gospel knowledge to meet it. Or the need I see may be disease or ignorance or bad housing, and I may have the medical, educational or social expertise to relieve it. To see need and to possess the remedy compels love to act, and whether the action will be evangelistic or social, or indeed political, depends on what we 'see' and what we 'have'.

This does not mean the words and works, evangelism and social action, are such inseparable partners that all of us must engage in both all the time. Situations vary, and so do Christian callings. As for situations, there will be times when a person's eternal destiny is the most urgent consideration, for we must not forget that men without Christ are perishing. But there will certainly be other times when a person's material need is so pressing that he would not be able to hear the gospel if we shared it with him. The man who fell among robbers needed above all else at that moment oil and bandages for his wounds, not evangelistic tracts in his pockets! Similarly, in the words of a missionary in Nairobi quoted by Bishop John Taylor, 'a hungry man has no ears' (p 37). If our enemy is hungry, our Biblical mandate is not to evangelize him but to feed him (Romans 12:20)! Then too there is a diversity of Christian callings, and every Christian should be faithful to his own calling. The doctor must not neglect the practice of medicine for evangelism, nor should the evangelist be distracted from the ministry of the word by the ministry of tables, as the apostles quickly discovered (Acts 6).

The Great Commandment

Let me return now to the Great Commission. I have tried to argue that its Johannine form, according to which the church's mission is to be modelled on the Son's, implies that we are sent into the world to serve, and that the humble service we are to render will include for us as it did for Christ both words and works, a concern for the hunger and for the sickness of both body and soul, in other words, both evangelistic and social activity. But supposing someone remains convinced that the Great Commission relates exclusively to evangelism, what then?

I venture to say that sometimes, perhaps because it was the last instruction Jesus gave us before returning to the Father, we give the Great Commission too prominent a place in our Christian thinking. Please do not misunderstand me. I firmly believe that the whole church is under obligation to obey its Lord's commission to take the gospel to all nations. But I am also concerned that we should not regard this as the only instruction which Jesus left us. He also quoted Leviticus 19:18 'you shall love your neighbour as yourself', called it 'the second and great commandment' (second in importance only to the supreme command to love God with all our being), and elaborated it in the Sermon on the Mount. There He insisted that in God's vocabulary our neighbour includes our enemy, and that to love means to 'do good', that is, to give ourselves actively and constructively to serve our neighbour's welfare.

Here then are two instructions of Jesus – a great commandment 'love your neighbour' and a great commission 'go and make disciples'. What is the relation between the two? Some of us behave as if we thought them identical, so that if we share our gospel with somebody, we consider we have completed our responsibility to love them. But no. The Great Commission neither explains, nor exhausts, nor supersedes the Great Commandment. What it does is to add to the requirement of neighbour-love and neighbour-service a new and urgent Christian dimension. If we truly love our neighbour we shall without doubt share with him the good news of Jesus. How can we possibly claim to love him if we know the gospel but keep it from him? Equally, however, if we truly love our neighbour we shall not stop with evangelism. Our neighbour is neither a bodyless soul that we should love only his soul, nor a soulless body that we should care for its welfare alone, nor even a body-soul isolated from society. God created man, who is my neighbour, a body-soul-in-community. Therefore, if we love our neighbour as God made him, we must inevitably be concerned for his total welfare, the good of his soul, his body and his community. Moreover, it is this vision of man as a social being, as well as a psycho-somatic being, which obliges us to add a political dimension to our social concern. Humanitarian activity cares for the casualties of a sick society. We should be concerned with preventive medicine or community health as well, which means the quest for better social structures in which peace, dignity, freedom and justice are secured for all men. And there is no reason why, in pursuing this quest, we should not join hands with all men of good will, even if they are not Christians.

To sum up, we are sent into the world, like Jesus, to serve. For this is the natural expression of our love for our neighbours. We love. We go. We serve. And in this we have (or should have) no ulterior motive. True, the gospel lacks visibility if we merely preach it, and lacks credibility if we who preach it are interested only in souls and have no concern about the welfare of people's bodies, situations and communities. Yet the reason for our acceptance of social responsibility is not primarily in order to give the gospel either a visibility or a credibility it would otherwise lack, but rather simple uncomplicated compassion. Love has no need to justify itself. It merely expresses itself in service wherever it sees need.

'Mission', then, is not a word for everything the church does. 'The church is mission' sounds fine, but it's an overstatement. For the church is a worshipping as well as a serving community, and although worship and service belong together they are not to be confused. Nor, as we have seen, does 'mission' cover everything God does in the world. For God the Creator is constantly active in His world in providence, in common grace and in judgment, quite apart from the purposes for which He has sent His Son, His Spirit and His church into the world. 'Mission' describes rather everything the church is sent into the world to do. 'Mission' embraces the church's double vocation of service to be 'the salt of the earth' and 'the light of the world'. For Christ sends His people into the earth to be its salt, and sends His people into the world to be its light (Matthew 5:13-16).

Towards Integrated Development

by The Rev George Hoffman

Jesus said, "I am come that they may have life, and have it more abundantly" (John 10:10), or, as the New English Bible translates it, "Life in all its fullness". If we are concerned to follow in the steps of our Lord Jesus Christ, we too must come to people prepared to share this life "in all its fullness".

As Christians for whom the Bible is authoritative, we have just as much (if not more) right to be concerned for man's total development as anyone. Unfortunately in the debate on development, the evangelical voice has seldom been heard, largely through our own default, and once again we have retreated from, if not wholly evacuated, yet another area where we have let other Christian and non-Christian voices and programmes dominate the scene, preoccupied with man's "horizontal" development at the expense of being concerned for man's total development – yet another casualty perpetuated by the false dichotomy between the so-called "social" and "spiritual" gospels. Dr Visser t'Hooft, in his retiring speech as General Secretary of the World Council of Churches, put it succinctly at the Uppsala Assembly, "A Christianity which has lost its vertical dimension has lost its salt, and is not only insipid in itself, but useless to the world. But a Christianity which would use the vertical dimension as a means to escape from responsibility for and in the common life of men is a denial of the incarnation of God's life for the world manifested in Christ".

Trevor Beeson has drawn attention to this unresolved tension between those who emphasise the "horizontal" ministry and those who emphasise the "vertical" ministry. And he laid the blame on "the absence of an adequate theology to undergird the great programme of social action". As evangelicals, surely we believe that we have such a theology. The question is, have we the compassion? And have we the concern to match such a theology?

Good Citizens

In his book 'On Being the Church in the World', Dr Robinson focuses attention on God's rule throughout society, and our role within that society. Referring to Paul's use of the word *Politeia* (citizenship) in his Epistle to the Philippians, he sees significance in the fact that although a Christian's ultimate "citizenship" is in heaven, Paul recognises the

89

importance of our citizenship here on earth. For in Phil 1:27, the Apostle uses the same word when he refers to our "manner of life" within society. A more suitable translation could in fact read "behave worthily as citizens". Consequently, John Robinson argues that there is no department of the world's life into which we as Christians are not commissioned to go. "They find themselves concerned with evangelization and with civilisation". In other words, "being worthy of the Gospel of Christ" means not only a concern for evangelization, it also involves a concern for civilisation. It was no doubt with this understanding in mind, together with his breadth of vision for the whole of God's world, that Dr Billy Graham wrote in his book 'World Aflame', "We as Christian citizens have no right to be content with our social order until the principles of Christ are applied to all men".

Bringing Deliverance

Now the Lausanne Congress on World Evangelization took for its mandate the words recorded in Luke's Gospel, chapter 4, where Jesus states that He is commissioned to preach the good news to the poor, to proclaim release to the captives, and recovery of sight to the blind, and to set at liberty those who are oppressed. If we are to make this mandate meaningful we must of necessity meet people as Jesus did, at their point of need. For if we consider each of these specific injunctions and see how Jesus expounded and explained them, both in His teaching and ministry to people in their need, the social implications of the Gospel will drive us to social involvement for the sake of the Gospel.

In 'One World – One Task', the report of the British Evangelical Alliance Commission on World Mission, there is an appendix on Christian Mission and Christian service. There Andrew Walls draws attention to God's creation mandate to subdue the earth and care for its inhabitants. "The proper use of the planet is therefore the direct concern of the Christian as a man in Christ: it is part of his obedience as man". Mr Walls goes on to say, "Questions of world poverty, of world food supply, of all the vast infrastructure of health, medicine, education, and government which undergird it, are his direct concern because God has so instructed man, and because they are duties of man as man".

If, then, we are going to take seriously the words of our Lord Jesus Christ, and bring deliverance to the captives, it will embrace deliverance from the constant threat of exploitation; deliverance from the indignity of a lifetime of servitude and unemployment; deliverance from the menace of death by starvation and malnutrition; deliverance from the threat of disease and chronic ill health through insanitary living conditions and the degrading squalor of some of our urban ghettos. These must all be seen as part and parcel of bringing deliverance to the captives of poverty, injustic, exploitation, and neglect. To talk and speak of just a "spiritual deliverance" is to truncate and devalue the glorious Gospel of our Lord Jesus Christ. And argues Canon Michael Green in 'Runaway World', "Unless Christians share His love for people, His hatred of poverty and disease and ignorance no less than sin, then their religion is not the religion of Jesus, whatever they may claim".

Remember the Poor

In his book, 'The Social Conscience of the Evangelical', Sherwood Eliot Wirt declares that the whole Bible could be considered from the sociological viewpoint as a defence of the poor. A casual glance at a concordance makes it abundantly clear that God has a continuing concern for the poor, a concern which He discharges through His people. It was a concern that became incarnate in Christ. The very fact that the poor had a share in the Gospel was one of the Messianic signs that He told the disciples to share with John the Baptist.

When the church sent out Barnabas and Paul on their mission to the Gentiles, the one and only obligation they laid upon them to "remember the poor", "Which very thing" said Paul, "I was eager to do".

Echoing the words of Deut 15:11, Jesus reminded us that we shall always have the poor with us, and "whenever you will, you can do good to them" (Mark 14:7). "By implication", says Hendriksen commenting on the parallel passage in John 12:8, "Jesus is saying to the Church of all ages that the care of the poor is its responsibility and privilege". And along with the responsibility and privilege there is the threatened judgment and reward recorded in Matthew 25. And it is no good looking for an escape clause in confining the words of our Lord either to a previous dispensation or to a narrowly circumscribed Christian community. As John Calvin says in his commentary on Matthew 25:45, "Christ is either neglected or honoured in the persons of those who need our assistance. So then, when we are reluctant to assist the poor, may the Son of God come before our eyes, to whom to refuse anything is a monstrous sacrilege".

The Dividing Gap

Faced with the fact that three-quarters of the world's population have to exist on a quarter of the world's wealth, Colin Morris' eloquent plea 'Include Me Out', forecasts a revolution that will convulse the planet and "expose our present ferment in the church as the gentle eccentricity of those who pick the flowers on the slopes of a rumbling volcano". The developing countries have now become convinced that the continuation of suffering from hunger, ignorance, disease, and injustice is not inevitable. At the Third World Medical Conference on Medical Education it was stated that "They no longer believe it is a rule of nature, or a law of God that they should be born to misery and hasten to an early grave". This is the spirit that won political independence for over 700 million people in Asia and Africa in the last three decades. They want freedom, but they also want food and homes and health and work and play. They no longer want the world to be divided, as an Indian writer has said, "between people whose vocabulary includes the word 'holiday', and the rest".

In Psalm 146 God's roles as Provider for the poor and Defender of the poor are put in juxtaposition by accident. "Happy is he whose help is the God of Jacob, who executes justice for the oppressed, who gives food to the hungry" (verse 7). And there are many who argue that throughout the emerging nations, the hungry will never be given adequate food until justice for the oppressed has been executed in their land.

Take South America, for example: the economic sickness of Latin America is aggravated by the fact that ten per cent of the population controls 90 per cent of the land. In Brazil, for instance, two thousand people own land enough to make collectively a territory larger than the combined area of Italy, Holland, Belgium and Denmark. The root of the trouble in many Latin American republics is the fact that the aristocracy constitutes an "establishment" power pattern which, often reinforced by the established church, is tied in with government. The effect is that in many countries society stagnates rather than develops and human life is degraded by hunger and disease. Millions of people are denied the opportunity of realising their potential as human beings (i e the quest for the *Humanum* — to use the words of the secular theologian) and of participating fully and genuinely in the life of society.

To deal with the root of this problem, many would argue that the socio-economic system must be changed. The imbalance must be rectified. New and more just relationships between rich and poor must be created. To change the system, to put right the imbalance between rich and poor is the responsibility of those who hold power and those who can influence that power, to ensure that the system be changed. To bring pressure to bear on those who wield power is then the responsibility of all who believe in justice and human rights. In his book 'Don't Sleep Through the Revolution', Dr Paul Rees quotes Ruben Lores, formerly of the Latin American Mission and one of the pioneers of Evangelism-in-Depth. "Today all over Latin America there is turmoil for a change not only of the conditions but of the patterns. We must have either accelerated political evolution or a chaotic revolution".

Of course there are those who read about the Maoist infiltration into East Africa and the Marxist insurgents in South America, and dismiss these particular problems of the developing countries as an exaggerated Communist plot. But it is both irresponsible and dangerously naive to dismiss the social and political unrest of the so-called 'Third World' as simply the work of the Communists. "If our social insights go no deeper than that", says Dr Paul Rees, "we are re-enacting Rip Van Winkle – sleeping through a revolution". Therefore, I believe we need to state along with Samuel Escobar that although evangelicals respect the state and the structures in which they live, we are not afraid of change, nor do we link the destiny of the church to the subsistence of particular forms of social and political organisation. Dr John Stott reminds us in 'Christ the Controversialist' that it has "Not been characteristic of evangelicals in the past to be shy of social action or even, when necessary, of political action".

The Quest for Justice

We need to recognise what the Old Testament teaches; namely that one of the characteristics of a society which has rejected God's laws is injustice. And one of the roles of the prophets speaking in God's name and on behalf of God's people was to condemn injustice, exploitation, and the abuse of power. In the face of the present situation, is this role any less reduced today? It is no good just loving a man condemned to a life sentence of poverty and oppression, while at the same time we remain silent regarding those factors which are responsible for them. "Love is not a substitute for justice", said Leighton Ford speaking at the US Congress on Evangelism in Minneapolis, "and since not all men are or will be converted to Christ, and since even we Christians have imperfect love, we have a responsibility to seek justice in society".

The Foreign Minister of Tanzania said the future of Christian churches in Africa would be determined by the way they defended justice, freedom and human rights, and so created conditions for peace. Opening a conference of senior Anglican clergy in Africa he questioned why the church had not condemned outright apartheid, colonialism, and exploitation in Africa. And he asked, "Is it simply that the church is blind to injustice"?

But in our quest for Justice one of our distinguishing marks as Christians must be a concern for people and not particular political theories. Archbishop William Temple pointed out in his introduction to 'Christian Social Reformers of the 19th Century', that Shaftesbury, like Wilberforce, was stirred by sympathy for individuals. "He had no theories about the Rights of Labour or any such abstractions. He was no democrat, and he actively disliked Trade Unions. But his conscience protested at the conditions under which men, women and above all, children were working in the factories. So he became the pioneer of factory legislation, deliberately invading the sphere of industrial and economic organisation in the name of humanity and at the dictation of Christian faith". The world cried out for such Christ-like invaders today.

If we really are concerned, then, to extend "the abundant life" as Jesus expounded it, we shall have to grapple far more seriously and strenuously with those factors in society which prevent men from enjoying life in all its fullness. We shall have to give far more attention to causes instead of being preoccupied with effects – with the disease more than with the symptoms. Although we shall always be called, as Jesus was, to render 'first aid' to the casualties of a sick society, we must be more prepared to speak out and to influence those things which cause corruption, prejudice, and victimization within our societies. Jesus did. And so must we if we are to follow in His footsteps.

"You give them something to eat"

Over 250 years ago, Jonathan Swift stated "Whoever could make two ears of corn or two blades of grass to grow upon a spot of ground where only one grew before, would deserve better of mankind and do more essential service to his country than the whole race of politicians put together". An overstatement? Maybe in the comparison. But surely not in the sentiments expressed – especially when one regards the conditions prevalent in the modern world.

A report in the 'New Internationalist' stated that "The world's food is so precariously balanced that one more season of shortage could lead to global disaster." Already seventeen countries of the world face serious or perennial food shortages, and another thirteen are in danger of shortages. And it is estimated the total number of people affected is 950 million, about one-third of the world's total population.

Meanwhile Jesus still says to His followers through His Word, "You give them something to eat" (Matt 14:16). If we are to redress the imbalance in the world to meet the basic need of man, as well as obeying the teaching of our Master, we shall have to divert our energies and potential resources to developing and preserving our neglected agricultural potential throughout the world. As Rene Padilla stated in his paper to the Lausanne Congress, "There is no place for statistics on how many souls die without Christ every minute, if they do not take into account how many of those who thus die, die victims of hunger".

According to A H Boerma, the Director General of the Food and Agricultural Organisation, the world food situation is more difficult than at any time since the years immediately following the devastation of the second world war. In a period when the world's population increased by 75 million mouths, world food production has actually declined. This is the startling and disturbing conclusion that the FAO comes to in one of its reports. And if up until now it has been easy for the developed countries to dismiss food shortage as not their problem, the FAO points out that for the first time in years the developed countries are going short as well.

In Psalm 63 the psalmist praises God for visiting the earth and watering it. He is acknowledged as the God of the whole world, "who greatly enriches it". But, the riches that God intends to be shared by everyone, have been hoarded and squandered, devastated and destroyed by a minority. While God on the other hand enriches the earth, it is man who through his selfishness has impoverished it and limited its resources. Nearly 70 per cent of the people living throughout the developing countries depend upon agriculture for their livelihood and by 1985 this number is expected to increase to nearly 90 per cent. And yet between one-third and one-half of the world's population suffers from malnutrition while only ten per cent of the world's arable land is actually cultivated.

In our socio-economic programmes therefore a much higher priority must be given to rural development with the utilisation of intermediate technology at the local level. In these programmes people must be helped to help themselves recognising that the success of any programme is directly proportional to the amount of local input in the way of planning, indigenous materials, assumed responsibility and willingness to work.

Take the 'Faith and Farm' project in Nigeria, for example. It is geared primarily for the farmer and his household who make up 95% of the population of Nigeria. The aim of this highly successful project is to train African Christians to teach other farmers and their families to recognise that Jesus Christ is Lord of every part of their lives. As a result, starchy, low-yielding crops have been replaced by nutritional foods with reinforced proteins. Inefficient hand-tools have been replaced by more practical instruments. Harvested crops have been properly stored and protected from the ravages of white ants and other termites. But more. Children sick and dying from disease and malnutrition have been given a new lease of life by a regular reinforced diet, and thousands of unemployed school-leavers have been given not only useful occupations but a new-found dignity and a fulfillment in a rewarding enterprise.

Interest in Everyday Problems

In the northeast area of Nigeria, where the work has been extended, one incident took place which is not in isolation, and serves to illustrate the evangelistic by-product of this kind of programme. One of the Faith and Farm agents saved the grain store of a Muslim and his family and protected his valuable millet and guinea corn against destruction and white ants. This was all the food that the family had for the year. Quietly the African Christian farmer shared his skill and knowledge as he worked alongside the Muslim farmer in preserving his crops. Later the Muslim inquired "What makes you give up your time and come to help me?" The farmer replied, "Because we want to be like our Master, Jesus Christ, who fed the people when they were hungry". And that day the Muslim farmer listened with sympathy to the Gospel message for the first time and he began to understand it. Another Faith and Farm worker explained that the better yields on his own farm were due to the powder he mixed with the seed before sowing in order to keep the insects away. His pagan neighbour agreed to try it for himself. It worked. And a venture developed because the pagan neighbour began to learn that the Christian God, through His servants, is interested in his everyday problems.

In another area of Africa a group of Christians in Western Dahomey realised that to stay on their over-populated, worn-out land was not honouring to God; furthermore as one leader expressed it, to continue working hard and getting practically nothing for it brought you to the point where you began doubting your own ability. Next to go, he added, was your self respect. They moved therefore to an area about a hundred kilometres away and soon found themselves welcoming non-Christians to the settlement. Within a short time, nearly all the strangers had become Christians. So began a movement that has proved to be as much an evangelistic enterprise as an agricultural one, with some school leavers seeing for the first time a future in the type of farming the settlement offered. Before long there were nine of these settlements, each started by a small group of Christians which grew as more people joined them.

Our development programmes, then, must be more comprehensive and inter-related, crossing the traditional lines of demarcation. For instance, we can help a man to grow more food, but that is of little value if we do not teach him how to store that food without much of it being eaten by insects. We can teach a man how to grow food of better nutritional value, but there is little point to it if we neglect to show him how to make sure that the water he drinks is free from disease.

Development with Dignity

It has been said that when a man has lost his dignity he has lost everything. And that is the first thing he loses when he becomes unemployed. He loses the respect of his neighbours. He loses the respect of his family. But worse. He loses respect for himself. This is one of the major sociological problems in the aftermath of disaster or national upheaval. But here, as in so many other areas, "man's extremity becomes God's opportunity".

In one rehabilitation programme in Bangladesh we had the privilege of supporting New Zealand missionary, Peter McNee. In the course of eighteen months he built over 1,200 houses in the Chandpur district that had been devastated by the civil war. But not only did he rehouse whole communities – he helped to restore their dignity by helping them to help themselves. The houses built cost no more than £50 each, because the local people rebuilt their own houses with timber and corrugated sheeting purchased by Tear Fund under the supervision and direction of Peter McNee who taught more than twenty local Bengali carpenters with his "on-the-job-training" techniques. In the course of the programme the Bengali foreman who was Peter McNee's right-hand man was soundly converted to Christ through what he saw in the life as well as through what he heard from Peter's lips.

"Give a man a fish and you feed him for a day", says the Chinese proverb. "Teach him how to fish and you feed him for life". We were able to prove the wisdom of this philosophy in that same area of Bangladesh. Utilizing the local jute products, we helped to restore the dignity of whole communities of unemployed Bengalis by teaching them how to make jute handicrafts. In one village the programme was introduced with seven pence worth of jute: soon the village was self-supporting with a turnover of £250 worth of goods per month.

An overriding concern then, for the dignity of man gives motivation to our involvement in the working conditions of men and the provision for the unemployed who are often the victims of a corrupt society or the unfair distribution of wealth within that society. Referring to the situation in India, P.T. Chandapilla, General Secretary of the Union of Evangelical Students of India said, "Evangelicals must do something more than they have ever done to affect the political and economic progress of national development. In the area of national commitment evangelicals are quite backward. Either they live in India as citizens of heaven, or with loose feet longing for citizenship in some western country". Sad to say, those words are not confined to India: they are universal.

Functional Literacy

One of the major factors regarding the growth and development of large communities in developing countries is the widespread illiteracy. But in tackling this particular problem, one recognises a basic mistake that we have made in the past and which must not be repeated in the future. Literacy must be seen as a means to an end, and not an end in itself. Ultimately it can do far more harm than good to impart, or at times impose, our more sophisticated patterns of academic education *per se.* All we succeed in doing is making dissatisfied people into educated people but still dissatisfied, because we have failed to relate their education to life. One still hears humorous (or horrifying?) stories of rural schools in Africa where they are taught unmeaningful geographical facts about a world outside they will never see or meet, and at the same time are left ignorant of how to develop their own land, raise their animals, tend their crops, and care for their family. Functional literacy, or work-orientated literacy, is one of the greatest needs we must be prepared to give time to, if we really are concerned to make men whole and are going to tackle the cause of the problem and not just treat the symptoms.

In his book 'Mission in the Seventies', Dennis Clark points out "educators now realise that the thousands of unemployable college graduates in India or Pakistan would have been better equipped with a technical school preparation, a business course, or agricultural training".

Functional literacy not only serves to meet the needs of the community, it gives motivation which is often lacking through disenchantment of seeing the effects – or lack of lasting effects – from the old academic literacy system which has been responsible for creating ghettos of educated but unemployed dissidents. Functional literacy very simply seeks to identify the local and immediate problems of a community, and gear its visual aids, vocabularies, and primers to solving those problems.

As the people outline their difficulties and begin to discuss the possible answers, they will then see their need for a certain amount of literacy work. They will see the need to understand diagrams, to count, and to work out simple calculations for the area of their land – for instance, the number of plants required, and how much feed is required to keep their cattle or poultry healthy. These very practical and down-to-earth matters help them to recognise the value of becoming literate and to put into practice what they are learning.

Joseph Jibi, the leader of a Faith and Farm project in Nigeria, wrote, "People have to be taught not only how to grow their vegetables, but also how to use them. Only when they understand the importance of fruit and vegetables in their diet will people come to use them in every day life".

No Wealth without Health

Benjamin Disraeli, once said that the wealth of a nation lay in the health of her people. In a day when the World Health Organisation informs us that 100 million people die or are disabled every year in developing countries because of a shortage of people with even the most elementary medical training, we cannot look upon medical ministry merely as an avenue for evangelism – a means to an end. It is part and parcel of the church's total mission, that is, if we are to be true to the commission and example of our Master, "who went about doing good and healing all that were oppressed by the devil" (Acts 10:38). It was part of His tripartite ministry that is clearly spelled out in Matt 9:35, where we are told that "Jesus went about all the cities and villages, teaching in their synagogues and preaching the gospel of the Kingdom, and healing every disease and infirmity". As Dr Kenneth Scott argues in 'The New Era in Medical Missions', medical missions are not a superfluous or even an accessory responsibility of the organised Christian world. They are fundamental, along with preaching and teaching.

A missionary doctor, writing from West Africa, believes that the first thing he has to offer that will be seen and accepted is his professional ability and integrity, "That is what we are expected to have", he writes. From that point slowly we may hope to proceed. When there is respect, one can expect liking to come in, and then, the Lord willing, fellowship and Christian love". At another conference I had the privilege of sharing in, a young missionary doctor shared with the conference some of the questions he had been forced to ask himself in his medical work in East Africa relating to public health programmes and the setting up of a 'Kwashiorkor' clinic. At first he had been plagued by the question, "Am I being a missionary? How many people am I winning for Christ"? This he argued was leading him up a cul-de-sac, until the Lord spoke to him and gave him peace in his own heart, helping him to see "that I was doing it because the Lord had commanded me to be compassionate, and I knew he wanted me to be a doctor. I am not just doing medical missionary work", he said, "in order to win people for Christ, but to care for people for the sake of Christ". And I thought later of something that Samuel Escobar wrote in his 'Social Responsibility and the Church in Latin America', when he took some Christians to task for having a guilty conscience over their schools and hospitals and health centres. "If in them we evangelise, splendid; but let us not use them", he argued, "as a medium of coercion to force upon others the Gospel. It is not necessary. In themselves, they are the expression of Christian maturity". Life in all its fullness, then, cannot be proclaimed *in vacuo* – neglecting the command and the example of our Lord Jesus Christ, who brought 'wholeness' to people who were in need of healing. But let us not fall into the trap of looking upon this ministry as a disguised form of evangelism, for as John Taylor rightly concludes in his book 'For all the World', "There is nothing in the Gospel that suggests either that Jesus healed men, or that He gave His healing powers to others, in order to make disciples". His healing ministry was an extension of His total mission and an expression of His love. Love without strings, "Not just in word or in speech, but in deed and truth".

The Whole Gospel to the Whole Man

In this sketchy and all too inadequate glance at some of the social implications of the Gospel, I have tried, by way of illustration, to underline what Senator Mark Hatfield states in his collection of addresses, 'Conflict and Conscience', where he argues very clearly that we must find viable means to relate the good news to the turmoil of our era. We must see, with him, that there is no point in wasting time and energy answering questions that nobody is asking. There is no purpose in harnessing our talents today to fight the theological battles of yesterday at the expense of the real socio-theological problems that will confront us tomorrow. "As we have addressed ourselves to the theological problems of organic evolution in the past", says Senator Hatfield, "Let us turn to the theological problems of social revolution in the present. To do less is to concern ourselves with only half of the Gospel".

Moreover, living in our 'global village' with its increasingly interlocking cultures and network of communications, our societies themselves are becoming increasingly inter-dependent. So too must our ministry. Again, as Senator Hatfield puts it, "We as evangelicals must regain sensitivity to the corporateness of human life. We must become sensitive to issues of social morality as well as to issues of private morality. We must learn to repent of and respond to collective guilt as well as individual guilt. This becomes increasingly important as the structures of life become more interdependent and interrelated. An ethic which deals solely with personal morals is singularly inadequate if it fails to deal with war, poverty, and racial antagonism as well.

If as Christians we believe that we are called to "bear one another's burdens", we must know what it means to share one another's burdens. I recall that someone once asked Solon the great Greek lawmaker, how justice could be achieved in Athens. "It can be achieved", he replied, "if those people who are not directly affected by wrong are just as indignant about it as those who are personally hurt". May such indignation drive us to a more real fulfillment of our task in bringing fullness of life to those we seek to serve.

The Great Commission

Obeying the Great Commission Now and Tomorrow

by Max Warren (an extract from 'I believe in the Great Commission' published by Hodder and Stoughton)

The Gospel is for the whole man: for the whole of mankind: and it is addressed to the whole natural order. But within history, its progress towards its goal has had to be spelled out in varying ways, in different contexts.

In the early centuries it proceeded by infiltrating a dominant culture. Only a very few of its agents were wise, fewer still were noble. They were, indeed, the 'offscourings' of the world. But, in due course, they turned that world upside down.

During the next thousand years the shape of their task was different. They had to bring order out of chaos. In doing so, they created a civilisation.

Then came more than four centuries of exploration. This was a geographical feat, but it was much more. The explorers had also to discover the true relation of man to the natural order, and, as well, to trace the contours of man himself. In the process there were opened up for the first time, the possibilities of unity for mankind. Glimpses, even, could be caught of that "far-off divine event, to which the whole creation moves", the wider harmony of the whole universe. The last is no fancy for those who take Ephesians 1:10 and Colossians 1:20 seriously.

If those very rough generalisations may serve as showing the underlying task of Christians, individually and corporately, in the past, then perhaps the word, 'incarnation' may be allowed to denote the peculiar task of today and tomorrow.

The Gospel has now to be seen to 'become flesh', so that the first 'Becoming' is made contemporary. This task is threefold. First, this new becoming has to be seen as genuinely local in expression everywhere. Then no less, it has to be seen as having everywhere a family likeness, an influence making for unity. These are the congenial aspects of its task.

Much less congenial, in a world more hostile than for many centuries, it has to show that eternity is uncomfortably immediate. Man's treatment of man, and man's treatment of nature, are leading inexorably to disaster. Far from God being dead, it is man who will soon be dead if he does not start to take God seriously. The good news of the wrath of God has to be spelled out as the complement of the good news of His love. Such a spelling out once led to the Crucifixion. There is no reason to think that it may not lead the obedient to the same experience followed as it surely will be by a similar resurrection.

Obeying the Great Commission today and tomorrow will be no easier than in the past. Matthew 24, Mark 13, Luke 21, John 16:31-33, and the whole drama of the Passion Story, and the Book of the Revelation are part of the New Testament. They were not written in order to be explained away.

Meanwhile our present task, the task of all who would be obedient, takes its pattern now as ever from the Great Commission Himself. We have our calling made very clear in the first verse of Hebrews 3: "Therefore, brothers in the family of God, who share a heavenly calling, think of the Apostle and High Priest of the religion we profess, who was faithful to God who appointed Him." The apostleship of Jesus Himself finds frequent echo in the record of John. Two passages are particularly important for us. "This is the work that God requires: believe in the one whom He has sent" (John 6:29); and "As the Father sent me, so I send you" (John 20:21). The word translated 'sent' is the verbal form of the word, 'apostle'. The witness of the other Gospels shows that this was the underlying conviction of all the teaching of Jesus. He was the Apostle of God, sent into the world with a message from God, which message He was.

This word 'apostle, together with its verbal forms, runs like a gold thread through the New Testament. But, in practice, as a word, it is virtually confined today to a strictly limited ecclesiastical use. Its true English equivalent, the only one, is the word 'missionary', that is 'one sent on a mission with a message'. The word is now familiar in secular as well as religious contexts. This is a very great advantage, for it helps to disinfect this very great word from some of its less happy associations in the nineteenth century. In all that follows I will be using the word, 'missionary' with the scriptural significance of 'apostle' in mind, and always in ultimate relation to the Apostle and High Priest of our profession.

Because misunderstanding is sometimes almost woefully easy, we should be clear that the word, 'missionary' is to be understood as applying to anyone, anywhere, who is committed to obedience to the great commission. That obedience may, for most, be confined to their 'Jerusalem'. For some it may mean moving into neighbouring 'Judea'. Others, perhaps, will find themselves unexpectedly in some uncongenial 'Samaria'. Still others will go to 'the ends of the earth'. All should be knit together in prayer, for their work is one. It should also be clear that the words 'missionary' and 'mission' are not to be restricted to individuals. They are equally relevant to group obedience. Ideally, they should refer to every congregation and to the universal Church.

So far, I have written as a Christian of the West. From now on, all I write, I write as a Christian who may be a Japanese or an Arab, a Korean or an Indian, a Persian or a Filippino, a Chinese or an African, or as one of any race or nation to whom a Christian may belong. Let us then consider the word, 'missionary' and the life and work of such a one, or such a company under seven aspects.

The Missionary as Inquirer

If this aspect is put first, it is not because it is the most important, but because, in the sense in which it is used here, it is commonly neglected. Being an asker of questions means being curious about everything that affects the people whom the missionary is hoping to meet. These people live in a very practical world, in which their living is profoundly influenced by political, economic and social factors, of which even they themselves are not always aware. It is by being inquisitive about these matters that the missionary becomes their contemporary; and that is part of the meaning of 'incarnation'.

'Becoming flesh', in this fashion, implies being knowledgeable. It implies asking questions of people, but also of books and newspapers and the mass media. If we do not ask the questions we will get no answers at all.

A great commentator on the prophecy of Isaiah, George Adam Smith, is describing the political situation which lay behind Chapter 10:5-34. For Isaiah and his contemporaries it looked as if the Assyrians were certain to invade and capture and destroy Jerusalem. An atheism of fear was obsessing the people.

> "Isaiah's problem was thus the fundamental one between faith and atheism; but we must notice that it did not arise theoretically, nor did he meet it by an abstract proposition. This fundamental religious question — whether men are to trust in the visible forces of the world or in the invisible God — came up as a bit of practical politics. It was not to Isaiah a philosophical or theological question. It was an affair in the foreign policy of Judah."

The crucial point is that Isaiah saw foreign politics as involving moral judgments. This insight applies to all politics, national and local, as well as international. This illustration is susceptible of infinite adaptations. The missionary, in any situation, needs to be politically and socially sensitive to moral issues, and to help others to be the same.

This does not mean that he becomes an amateur politician. The missionary today, who serves in a country not his own, is very much a guest of the country as well as of the Church. He will quite certainly be viewed by some with a measure of suspicion as being politically unreliable. He will be watched. He owes it both to the country and the Church to be above suspicion as a meddler. That is why, the more alert he is to things as they are, the less likely he is to be taken by surprise by events. He will be immune to the atheism of fear, and will help to immunise others.

The Missionary as Learner

The word, 'disciple' means a learner, and the missionary remains a learner to the end. We have seen him asking questions. Now he has to learn what are the real questions which the people he meets are asking. The more he discovers of these questions, the less ready he will be to imagine that he knows all the answers.

To discover what are the real questions people are asking means learning their language. The language may be that of a strange people: or the language of a strange younger generation of his own race: often, it will be the language of those of his own generation trained to think in ways foreign to his own experience.

Learning a language so that you really understand it, think in it, even dream in it, is a physically, mentally, and spiritually exhausting experience. But if we are to transpose the message with which we believe we have been entrusted in a way which will be understood, there is no escape from learning how the other man is thinking. And that involves learning how he is 'feeling' and his 'feelings' are the fruit of his own cultural inheritance. The missionary has much to learn, particularly so if he crosses a cultural frontier.

Klaus Klostermaier comments on this last point; he tells how Hindu friends complained repeatedly that the Hindi of our Bible translation was no 'Hindi', but a 'foreign language'. The translators knew the grammar and dictionary, but not Hinduism. The logic of Klostermaier's plea was not less Hindi, but more. Unless and until we know a lot more about how Hindus use their own language, we shall never be able to use it ourselves so as to speak effectively and meaningfully about Jesus. That is authentic missionary experience.

There is some shrewd wisdom in a letter by a fourth-century writer, Evagrius, explaining to a friend about his translation of the life of St. Antony, which he has produced. He has had to translate from Greek into Latin, and he says —

> "Direct word for word translation from one language into another darkens the sense and strangles it, even as spreading couchgrass a field of corn ... For

my part to avoid this, I have so transposed this life of the Blessed Antony which you desired that whatever lack there may be in the words, there is none in the meaning. Let the rest go bat-fowling for letters and syllables: do you seek for the sense."

That is admirable advice for all missionaries, and particularly so for interpreters of the Bible.

Side by side with this care for learning the language, we need to be ever learning the implications of our common humanity. One contemporary phenomenon is the widespread emergence, especially among the young, of a growing consciousness of this underlying reality. Easily, it may lead to very superficial conclusions about all religious experience being equally valid, but it remains a very important phenomenon of our time. The 'hippie trail to the East' deserves understanding, for we, as Christians, believe that God's own image has been defaced, not destroyed, and that His purpose of a common salvation remains unchanged. That is our Christian conviction and the basis of our hope. Our realism can provide the corrective to superficial optimism by affirming the reality of our common sinfulness. As one missionary whom I know has put it — "This means that the dividing line between good and evil does not pass between the Christian on the one hand and the Hindu, Buddhist or Muslim on the other — which is what we have all too readily assumed in the past — but between all of us men and the searching judgment of the divine word." To learn that, for the missionary, will mean being very humble.

The Missionary as Listener

There is a listening which obviously belongs to learning a foreign language. Without a musical ear, without some facility in catching the nuances in a tonal language, it is almost impossible to learn some languages. But the listening with which I am concerned here is 'listening' to people. This may involve crossing the ocean, or just crossing the road.

Listening to another person is a great deal more of an art than most of us realise. The true listener is giving all his attention to what the other person is saying, listening even to his silences.

A subtler point still is, that as I so listen, I become aware of myself listening. This is important for, unless I listen to myself listening I will be likely to assume, quite wrongly, that a word used in the context of my own experience means the same as in the experience of the one to whom I am listening. There is much wisdom as well as a proper courtesy in this sensitivity of listening.

Furthermore, if we are listening 'in the name of Jesus Christ', we have to listen to Him as a partner in the conversation. This is not playing with words. For once we realise that He is listening, we must be ready to hear Him speaking. He may say something we have never heard before. Given our concentrated attention, we may hear Him speaking through the lips of the other person, be he an agnostic, a humanist, a Marxist, a Hindu, a Muslim, a Buddhist or a Jew — or anyone. This kind of listening can be very exciting. It is something every missionary must practise. Jesus, now as always, is very full of surprises.

The Missionary as Lover

Several times in this book we have had occasion to speak of the patience of God. Would we be so very wrong were we to say that patience is the greatest of all His attributes? For what is patience but love in action: love waiting; love suffering; love pursuing; love ever respecting our freedom, however much we abuse it? If this is the supreme attribute of God, it must be the supreme attribute of the missionary. He, if he knows himself, knows that he has already tried the patience of God to the limit. He must show to others what God has shown to him.

Applicable to all missionaries in every situation, across the world or across the street, are some words spoken by Bishop Stephen Neill to a missionary group many years ago when he was still a missionary in India. He knew well how often those to whom he was speaking, out of sheer love for some individual, tried to force the pace of his flowering into Christian faith. Speaking to himself and to the group, he said —

"Let us not mix up our affair and God's. It is our business to see that if possible the enquirer's face is turned to the light, and if possible that he is kept on the move. If he has left Ur of the Chaldees, that is the great thing. But it takes time to get all the way across the desert to the promised land; and it is our part to lose neither faith nor patience, but to emulate the patience of God."

That is a great parable. I quote another, this time from one of the nineteenth century pioneers in Iran, Dr. Bruce. Writing home, he described his work as follows — "I am not reaping the harvest; I scarcely claim to be sowing the seed; I am hardly ploughing the soil; but I am gathering out the stones. That too is missionary work, let it be supported by loving sympathy and fervent prayer".

There is no accident in that both parables suggest something of a desert. The missionary, now and always, is faced with a desert in which his calling is to "prepare a road for the Lord through the wilderness, clear a highway across the desert for our God" (Isaiah 40:3).

If I take these illustrations from Asia, that is by the way. The parables are equally relevant to the desert of the English Midlands, to Chicago, to the Ruhr or Amsterdam, to Sao Paulo, Lagos or Nairobi. Loving will take many forms, each of them, in a real sense, a sacrament. The minister of the sacrament may be a shop-steward on the floor of a factory: a management consultant; a doctor or a nurse in a hospital; a teacher opening windows in the minds of pupils; a translator pursuing an elusive word to give sense to what he is translating; the hostess whose home is ever open to any visitor; the man or woman struggling across the desert of learning a foreign language; that through them the Word made flesh may win His way and "pass the low lintel of the human heart".

Being a missionary, anywhere, is to be a lover. There is no other way.

The Missionary as a Link

The Christian Church exists all over the world. Its proportion, in relation to the total population, may be minute. In more places than one it is, for all practical purposes, proscribed. But it is there. In some places it is growing very fast indeed, though statistics are an unreliable yardstick of spiritual progress.

Now, the missionary, whose particular vocation it is to cross national or cultural frontiers, has a distinctive role besides any others which are here being considered. He, in a very special sense, is a sacrament of the universal Church. His presence is a visible assurance to the local Christian community that they are members of a world-wide fellowship. He can assure them that other Christians are remembering them in their prayers. Persevering in intercession is very difficult without some personal link with those for whom one intercedes. Further to this, the missionary has a unique role in interpreting that local community to their prayer-partners in the land from which he or she comes. This is a very responsible role indeed.

It must be looked for and hoped for and worked for, that the countries of the West from which, in the past, most missionaries to Asia and Africa and Latin America have come, will themselves be receiving missionaries from these other lands. They may not be 'wanted', they may even be resented, but they are certainly needed! Already, we know well the great value of visitors coming to Britain, for instance, from Asia and Africa, bringing with them the inspiration and challenge of their own discovery of Christ. But the visits are all too short. The day of the long-term missionary is, we hope, soon to dawn here.

'Long-term' is also still a relevant category for some missionaries from the West. All talk about a 'moratorium' on these foreign missionaries greatly over-simplifies a complex question. Commonly, such talk generalises from local situations where particular problems exist, and is rarely endorsed without many qualifications by the responsible leaders of the Churches of Africa and Asia.

An African from Kenya, with some slight exaggeration, recently put it thus — "World tourists cannot help the Church". To make clear what he meant, he went on to say — "Those who come must be people of God, ready to go along with others, to get submerged and to make mistakes; not tamed things, but those ready to initiate — partners in fact". The English may be sketchy, but the sense is clear!

That Kenyan commentary deserves careful study. Tourists do not get 'submerged'. Their mistakes are crudities which, at most, cause passing offence. They are not the mistakes from which lessons can be learnt. A tourist cannot be a 'partner' in the creative sense for which that African is asking.

A 'moratorium' on financial aid from abroad is another question altogether. It is, as with 'foreign missionaries', a proper subject for negotiation as between partners. It is no fit subject for facile generalisations.

Another factor which has to be kept in mind is the continuing danger for a local Church of its becoming introverted, and thus isolated from the broad stream of the Christian Faith, and coming to hold that Faith, not in 'due proportion' but in varying degrees of imbalance.

Besides this, it helps to demonstrate the catholicity of the national Church to have other nationals working alongside.

Again, an English Christian who resents an Asian immigrant being appointed as churchwarden in his parish church is as spiritually irresponsible as an Asian Christian who objects to a foreign missionary holding any office in the local Church. One of them may be a racialist, the other a nationalist; both, in their reactions, are sub-Christian.

The Missionary as Disturber

The parable of the leaven (Matt 13:33) was concerned to make one special point which is frequently missed. The peculiar property of leaven is that it causes fermentation. What our Lord is saying is that the Kingdom of Heaven, by its very existence as a Society, sets up a ferment, excites attention, which may be very disturbing indeed.

Consider a typical illustration, to which innumerable parallels can be found. A Christian from the Southern Sudan goes to Omdurman in the overwhelmingly Muslim Northern Sudan. He and his fellow-Christians from the South have proved to be a considerable surprise. Some Muslims have been so impressed by the lives of the despised Christians from the South that they find their way to Christian worship, causing thereby no small ferment, from which much may grow. That is our Lord's parable in action.

Wordsworth's joy, his "sense sublime of something far more deeply interfused" began with "a presence that disturbs". Any missionary presence is meant to be disturbing. Liberating men's spirits from the bondage of sin: their minds from the bondage of ignorance; their bodies from the bondage of hunger and disease: this may set up a mighty ferment indeed.

The Missionary as a 'Sign of the End'

"The Christian hope is a frontier subject and uses a frontier-language". In saying this, the late Bishop Fison gives us a clue to many passages in the Bible which are very puzzling if they are taken literally. He also offers us another clue in an illuminating phrase, 'lovers' time', which is how he interprets some of the sayings of Jesus about 'eternal life' — that it is a timeless experience as, for example, "This is eternal life: to know Thee who alone art truly God, and Jesus Christ whom Thou hast sent" (John 17:3).

It is in some such way that we are to understand the words of Jesus as reported by Matthew (24:14) — "This gospel of the kingdom will be proclaimed throughout the earth as a testimony to all nations; and then the end will come". This does not refer to some heavenly calendar for us to guess about. If ever words spoke of 'lovers' time', these do. And it is in this sense that the missionary is a 'Sign of the End'.

How strange it is that so many fail to challenge the wisdom, let alone the morality of exporting the instruments of physical death, while the export of a joy which conquers both death and sin is deplored as "forcing religion on people"!

The missionary, by virtue of that impulse of urgency to which he is a witness, invites men to feel the power of God's love; to face the necessity of choice, whether to respond to or reject it; to accept the burden of responsibility for others; to confront the reality of death.

All this he does today as though the work in which he is engaged will last a thousand years. He will bring every talent that he possesses to the task in hand as a skilled "master-builder ..." (1 Cor 3:10 ff). He is present for tomorrow. He plays his part in a society for whose redemption he prays and works and offers himself. He is consciously part of the ongoing process of history. He is, as any other good citizen, a builder of a better order. He is in this world, as our Lord prayed that he would be (John 17:15). At the same time, he knows both that human sin and selfishness can frustrate God's purpose, bringing all to ruin and destruction, and that he may have misjudged God's timing. More even than that, he knows that this day may be his last. He is a frontiersman who knows that the coming of God's Kingdom in its fulness, whatever its form in this world and the next, is in the hands of God. In both respects he is a man overflowing with hope, serving as he does the God of hope, who is "the source of all fortitude and all encouragement" (Rom 15:5,13). All this is only another way of affirming the fundamental emphasis of the New Testament that Jesus Christ is both present and coming.

In all these respects the missionary stands on the crucial frontiers of life. Through him the Holy Spirit "confutes the world and shows where wrong and right and judgment lie" (John 16:8). To be a missionary anywhere is to accept a formidable vocation.

Under all these seven aspects we are to view the missionary calling. No one of these characteristics is new. They have always been the proper equipment of the missionary. But they need to be minted afresh. They need to be seen to be what they are, the indispensable qualifications for Mission in the very difficult and, in some ways, novel circumstances of our time.

In so defining the word 'missionary' and describing his mission, whether in terms of the individual, the group, or the Church as a whole, no attempt is made here to argue for this form of missionary activity or that. We cannot foresee the future. What we do see is an extremely perplexing world. Ancient stabilities have disappeared. We cannot affirm with any certainty that the patterns of institutional Church life, as traditionally understood, will survive. They may do so. On the other hand, they have disappeared in China, and not only there. Long ago they disappeared in North Africa, and have not reappeared. Behind the Iron Curtain the Church lives in perpetual tension with the several governments. Economic factors alone could radically change the shape of the Church in the rest of the world. Again, the pattern of Mission-crossing-frontiers may have to take forms in sharp contrast to what was commonplace, even twenty-five years ago. Indeed, this is already happening as, increasingly, institutional activities are being taken over by governments, activities which were once the normal pattern of work. We can face all this without either alarm or despondency. All the seven aspects of the missionary which we have considered will continue to be relevant for Mission until that day when the Great Commission Himself will have seen the whole travail of His soul and is satisfied (Isaiah 53).

PART THREE:

Bible Study

Spiritual Warfare

A Bible Study by Miss M S Foote

Reality of Spiritual Warfare

Revelation 12:7-17 (especially 12)

Context of verse 12 — book
Written to churches facing persecution to strengthen and encourage believers to stand firm.
— chapter
Opposition of Satan and his demonic forces to God and His angelic hosts, especially to the
Lord Jesus Christ from the beginning (cf. vv 4—6 & 13—16 Old Testament people of God
give birth to Messiah: Satanic determination to exterminate the 'seed of the
woman' Gen 3:15): climax 12:5.
— verse
v 7 manifestation of Satan's power in spiritual warfare, unseen to us.
v 10 decisive victory over Satan of the Lord Jesus Christ.
vv 12, 17 concentration of all Satan's resources now on earth against Christians, not
because victorious by because defeated and knows his time of freedom is specifically
limited.

There is nothing new or unusual about spiritual warfare, Victory is assured and adequate
resources are available to God's people.

Ephesians 6:10—13 (especially 12 and 13)

Paul asserts—   reality of warfare,
                necessity of resistance,
                availability of resources for it.

Goal of Spiritual Warfare

Daniel 11:32

'Stand firm . . . take action' R S V
'Be strong   . . . do exploits' A V
Context
Age of turmoil, wars, tremendous suffering among nations; age of apostasy, confusion, persecution among God's people.
One group stands out – characterised by:
Stability = steadfast endurance
Capacity for wise, effective action among all the pressures = victorious counter-attack.
Drawing on resources producing endurance and effectiveness

Resources of Spiritual Warfare

'the people who know their God' – First resource and the most vital one

Knowledge of God

Ephesians 3:14–21

Goal of Paul's prayer in context of Ephesus (Acts 19:11-20, especially 19)
   a knowledge of love of Christ
   b experience of the fulness of God
   c glory – exaltation of the Lord Jesus Christ because of God's power in Christ through us

Knowledge of God many-sided; aspect perhaps most challenged is the knowledge of the love of God in Christ; no substitute for basic, essential security of being deeply rooted in the love of God: –
   1 *Be sure of His love for you,* His acceptance of you as you are (not for what you are or may become, not for anything you can do) but just because He IS love, love from which nothing can separate you.
   2 *Be sure of His love for others,* His acceptance of them, just as they are . . . ie your fellow workers . . .
   3 *Be sure of His love for the multitudes* . . .
   4 *Be sure of His overall sovereignty,* His providential control, His wisdom. Mk 1:32–38; esp. 35 & 38. Example of the Lord Jesus Christ as a man amongst vast unmet need, at peace, unpressurised in the middle of it, because He was walking with His Father, sure of His Father's concern and compassion for them.

— We need to learn not to be overwhelmed by unmet need, by oppressive sense of evil, by natural reactions and feelings; not to withdraw in breakdown or callowness; but positively to affirm great facts of love of Christ.

— Use Scriptures, hymns etc. to help you praise and pray, off-loading the cares upon God.

Knowledge of God is a growing knowledge resulting in a growing security, it goes hand in hand with a growing knowledge of ourselves.

Knowledge of Ourselves and Others

Ephesians 3:16 (in context of verses 14–19)

Picture of strengthening of a building
This is a twofold process: –   discovering weak places,
                                shoring up and/or replacing with new parts
Such strengthening is essential preparation for, essential part of process of growth, if we are to know 'filling with all the fulness of God', with His love, His power, His resources.

A Importance, therefore, of self-discovery — not introspection but openness to the Holy Spirit and to what He reveals to us as we read God's word, and in relationships and circumstances of life.
Ps 51:6   God's desire = 'truth in the inward being'
Jn 8:31, 32 & 36   God's desire for liberation of the human personality
Heb 4:12, 13   God's knowledge, comfort and security of it:
                 He is unshockable, we and others can never go beyond reach of His love.
Not introspection but humble, honest facing what Holy Spirit reveals, in expectant trust, and in deep security in His love.

B Self-discovery leads to acceptance: –
  1 *that you are a human being* . . . living, reacting, changing, therefore unpredictable, with weaknesses and limitations as well as strengths and gifts. So are other people.
  Therefore don't put on a façade yourself, don't live behind a mask, don't put others on a pedestal.
  2 *that you are a fallen human being, a sinful human being:* Therefore
  — you will react selfishly, thoughtlessly, aggressively, critically; so will others . . .
  — you will find yourself and others at times proud, touchy, jealous, irritable, fearful, withdrawn or aggressive even, and most often, over little things.
  3 *that you have the basic needs of a God-given human personality:* – spiritual, emotional, mental, physical — very closely interrelated.
    a *the need for significance,*
    having value, worth in and of yourself.
  Not wrong to need this, because significance is God's gift (cf creation narrative and its order . . . man the apex, highest point of God's creation, distinctive in a number of ways from rest of creation, made in the image of God.

You have the need for significance, ctd.

– under attack, threatened in all sorts of ways each time we enter a new, unknown environment:–

Who am I?	loss of identity	} therefore, have I any
Where do I fit in?	loss of relevance	} significance; any value?

b *the need of acceptance, a sense of belonging.*

again, God's gift; for Adam a special relationship with God and with Eve.

– this too, under attack, threatened in all sorts of ways:–

because there is much I cannot understand   – folk too busy to explain.
                                                folk too weary to explain.
because there is much I cannot communicate   – no language; turmoil of feelings
                                                and reactions.
because there is much I cannot do, I may feel rejected by fellow-workers set in their ways; rejected by those I'm trying to help and wonder why I ever came.

c *the need for purpose or achievement,* work to do which brings a satisfactory sense of achievement –

again God's gift – Genesis mandate to have dominion over the earth.

– under attack, threatened in all sorts of ways:–

only a drop in the bucket of unmet need.
only a very inadequate drop, mitigating, not curing.
limited and frustrated in all sorts of ways.
no time to preach the gospel.
no ability to preach the gospel.

Therefore terrible sense of inadequacy and frustration, of failure and guilt.
(cf anchor of Micah 6:8 'live Christ')

Basic human needs, threatened in a new situation, with unknown and great pressures – Satan seeks to exploit them as bridgeheads leading to spiritual depression, paralysis, doubts, loss of faith in God, His existence, His love etc.

Holy Spirit intends to use situation to empty us of all false self-confidence or self-sufficiency, of all false dependence on people or things, to bring us into a new and fuller experience of God and His resources.

Knowledge of Our Enemy

Times of transition and crisis often intensify our awareness of spiritual warfare, bring out what we are really like (bits of us we didn't know existed – very disconcerting and devastating at times!), also increases our knowledge of the enemy.

A Know your enemy – but don't get obsessed by him

Satan delights to become the centre of attention, to be talked about, if he cannot be dismissed or ignored as non-existent – Christian focus is always on the Lord Jesus Christ.

Remember
1 *Christ created the principalities and powers*
Colossians 1:15–17
> Therefore Christ is greater than they are; they continue in existence at His will; no ultimate dualism in the universe.

2 *Christ has conquered the principalities and powers*
Colossians 2:13–15
> Satan and fallen angels are at enmity with God.

BUT – Christ in His death atoned for our sins, thereby robbed Satan of any claim over us.
– Christ in His ascension was exalted over all principalities and powers **(Eph 1:20, 21, 22)** and we in Christ share that position with Him **(Eph 2:5, 6)**

3 *Christians are still in conflict with the principalities and powers*
(Eph 6:12).
> Satan and his hosts oppose the Christian and his purposes, but he and they are defeated in principle.

B Learn to recognise your enemy
and the sort of activities characteristic of him: –

1 *Character and Characteristic Activities*
Illustrated by the titles he is given in Scripture.

a *Satan* = adversary
    inciting rebellion against God
    source of questions . . . why? why? why?
    'Why does God allow?'
    'Why shouldn't I?'
    – learn to ask 'am I part of the problem or part of the answer?'

b *devil* = accuser
    malignant slanderer
    out to destroy men and the church before God (cf Job)
    to make men destroy one another (Jn 8:44)

2 *Means used by Satan in these activities*

a *Deception*
Blinding man's mind to the truth, sowing seeds of distortion and unbelief.
Satan tries to deceive us: –
i regarding truth and doctrine in general 2 Cor 11:13–15
(leading to false view of God, unbelief in His goodness, love, justice)
(leading to false view of God's word)
ii regarding truth about himself –
(leading to extremes – disbelief in his existence and activity
                    finding demons behind every incident)
iii regarding our position in Christ as triumphant over Satan
(leading to false view of circumstances – discontent, grumbling, slander, gossip and false accusations)

b *Slander leading to schism*
Perpetual smear campaign against God and man.
Satan tries to divide us: — Causing splits, camps, schisms over non-essentials.

c *Temptation*
Satan tries to divert us: —
i from believing God's word — unbelief
ii from obeying God's will — disobedience
iii from walking God's way — backsliding
Three steps leading to self-indulgent uses of human appetites or false asceticism —
(cf importance of balance)

d *Depression*
Satan tries to depress us: —
i relying on feelings not facts, in matters of forgiveness, acceptance, spiritual strength.
ii direct attack = oppression of mind or body (something distinct from spiritual depression or clinical depression)

e *Demonic Activity*
Use of occult activities to bring and hold men in bondage — ('serpent' very subtle, disguised sometimes as angel of light = 'Lucifer')
Satan counterfeits, apes knowledge and power that belong to God alone, luring man to gain them by evil, forbidden means.

3 Satan as the god of this world

2 Cor 4:4   'the god of this world'
1 Jn 5:19   'the whole world is in the power of the evil one'
Eph 2:2   'the prince of the power of the air'
Holding men and territory under his control because man has given his allegiance to Satan; but no longer any right to do so, because defeated — man can be delivered 'from power of Satan unto God', reclaiming lives and territory.
Beware of underestimating Satan.
Beware of overestimating Satan.
Importance of spiritual discernment for right diagnosis and right counter measures.

Knowing Our Resources for Victory

Revelation 2, 3
Expectation of victory
Repeated promises made to 'He who conquers . . .'
Repeated statements made about 'He who conquers . . .'

Ephesians 1:20, 21:2:6
Sharing position of victor.

2 Corinthians 10:3-5
Possessing adequate weapons.

A Prerequisites for using our resources
Essential for effective use of our weapons

a *Committed Soldiers*
no known reservations – 2 Tim 2:3–6; Rev 12:11
no indiscipline indulged
no known enemy footholds that have not been repented of and dealt with
(including any occult influences)
NB Two basic principles:
i 1 Peter 5:8,9 following 6 – resist Satan in position of humble submission to God
ii 2 Tim 2:22 – flee temptation

b *Cleansed Soldiers*
Rev 12:11 ⎫
1 Jn 1:7   ⎬ NB i the word of God as a mirror and a liberating power (revealing sin, showing us what to do to be free from its guilt and power)
Jas 1:21–25 ⎭
Jn 8:31,32   ii the blood of the Lamb to cleanse and to silence the accuser.

c *Confident Soldiers*
no false confidence in human power or resources; absolute confidence in the Captain of our salvation and His sufficiency. Such confidence based in knowledge of our resources.

B Our Resources

a *Our Authority* – 'the Name of Jesus'
represents all that He is – personality, attributes –
represents all that He has done – power
– using His Name not repeating a magic formula, but acknowledging, affirming and claiming His God-given supreme authority over, and superiority to, all other powers in the universe of whatever sort –
   Phil 2:9–11
   Col 2:13–15
   Eph 1:20–23
   Lk 10:17–20 delegated authority, therefore, beware of pride.
– look up references in concordance under 'in the name . . . ' or 'in My name . . .'
(salvation, healing, exorcism, prayer. gift of Spirit, preaching, worship and discipline)
– BUT we can use His Name only for something that He would truly put His signature to.

b *Our Armour* – Ephesians 6:13–17

1 Nature of armour
'whole' – affording total provision for defence and attack
'of God' – provided, guaranteed by Him,
   I cannot contribute any part of it, can only take it and put it on – still feel pressures, blows etc but safe.
all for protection – except for sword of the Spirit also used offensively.

2 Use of armour

the girdle of truth to counter lies and errors.
cf The Lord Jesus Christ using truth of God's word, affirming it in the wilderness
temptations; "it is written" . . . NB He used commands in their context.

the breastplate of righteousness to counter evil and sinful desires.
they make us feel polluted — not sin if resisted; forgotten when forgiven, therefore
resist Satan's accusations.

feet shod with 'the equipment of the gospel of peace' to counter opting out
of warfare.
proclamation of gospel = a positive answer
(NB boots of Roman soldier gave him firm stand and mobility)

the shield of faith to counter unbelief in many, subtle and varied guises.
  ie loss of identity and worth — we matter to God because He created and
                                     redeemed us
                                    — we matter to others because they pray for us.
    loss of relevance and acceptance — here to give not to get.
    loss of purpose and achievement — results in God's hands; ours to obey
  — set sights realistically, focus on tiny bits of progress, success, pinpoints of light,
not on darkness, be alert to see His encouragements.

helmet of salvation to protect from calamity, accident and sickness
  — 'God's servant is immortal till his work is done'

the sword of the Spirit
  cf The Lord Jesus Christ's use of it — value of storehouse of Scripture
  'praying in the Spirit' — positively ask the Holy Spirit's help.

Remember
The Holy Spirit Himself in us from conversion; allow Him full control; expect Him to give
spiritual gifts in fellowship as needed.

Biblical View
of Occult Activities

Deuteronomy 18:9-12

Full catalogue of different types of occult practice covering all forms of satanic worship; attempts to contact the dead; discovering knowledge concerning the past, present or future by any supernatural means; all forms of witchcraft, magic, spiritism etc.

Leviticus 26: 39ff

Confession and renunciation of parental involvement in occult practices.

Leviticus 19:31/Isaiah 8:19 & 20/Isaiah 27:9 & 10

Forbidding of seeking the services of occult practitioners because this is apostasy from God as sovereign controller and guide.

Exodus 22:18

Death penalty for those using occult powers.

Leviticus 20:6/Isaiah 19:3 & 4

God's judgment on those seeking occult help = casting out of the individual from God's people; abandoning of the nation to the domination of the occult.

The NT assumes knowledge of this OT teaching.

Cases of Demon Possession ~ Guide Lines

No gift of exorcism in N.T. though a Jewish practice, demands a combination of gifts of discernment, faith and healing.

a   Seek advice of an experienced person and allow him to handle case if possible.
Don't be eager to be involved or used — if unavoidable, work in a group if at all possible

b   Preparation in prayer and fasting — put on armour.

c   Person should be willing to be ministered to and to renounce Satan and follow Christ.

d   Don't lay hands on person during exorcism — (not Biblical).

e   Challenge demon or demons in Name of the Lord Jesus Christ to state names and numbe
Forbid them in the Name of the Lord Jesus Christ to do any hurt or harm to the person
Bind the demon(s) in the Name of the Lord Jesus Christ and order him/them out).
Forbid re-entry into that or any other person: consign to place "reserved for you
for eternal judgment".

f   Help delivered person to commit himself to the Lord, seal off areas that gave Satan
foothold; claim fulness of the Holy Spirit with laying on of hands.

g   Beware of set pattern; phrases; pride.

Books dealing with Spiritual Warfare

David C K Watson - 'God's Freedom Fighters' - Send the Light
F D Leahy - 'Satan Cast Out' - Banner of Truth
Robert Peterson - 'Roaring Lion' - O M F
Robert Peterson - 'The Demon gods of Thorny River' - O M F
Raphael Gasson -'The Challenging Counterfeit' - Logos
Jessie Penn-Lewis -'War on the Saints' - The Overcomer Literature Trust

Poverty, Hunger and Justice

A series of twelve Bible study outlines prepared by Ronald Sider

1 God Sides with the Poor

God Sides with the Poor at the Pivotal Points of Revelation History

Main Texts: Exodus 6:2-9; Amos 4:1-3; Luke 4:16-20

Exodus 6:2-9

1   What different reasons are given for God's decision to liberate the Israelite people in Ex 6:2-9?

2   On the basis of these other texts, how central to God's purpose at the Exodus was the liberation of oppressed people? (Ps 103:6-7; Gen 15:12-14; Ex 3:7-10; Deut 26:1-11).

3   Why do you think it is especially black theologians and Latin American theologians who have seen this emphasis on liberation in the Biblical teaching on Exodus?

Amos 4:1-3

1   Why does the prophet denounce the comfortable, well-off ladies so harshly and predict terrible destruction?

2   What contact do you think the ladies (whose affluent lifestyles were possible because their husbands oppressed the poor) had with the poor? Who would be their equivalents in today's society?

3   Do the texts given below on the destruction of Israel and Judah show the God of the Exodus still at work with the same concerns? (Jer 22:1-5; Micah 2:1-10; Zeph 3:1; Zech 7:8-14; 1 Kings 21:1-19; Is 3:1-25; Jer 5:26-29; 7:1-15; 12:1-7; 22:13-19; Micah 3:1-12; 6:9-15; Amos 4:6-9; 6:4-6).

Luke 4:16-20

1   How does Jesus define his mission at this public event at the beginning of his ministry?

2   In Luke 7:18ff, John the Baptist asks if Jesus is the expected Messiah. How does Jesus' response (vv 21-22) correspond with Luke 4:16ff?

3   How does Jesus' definition of his mission correspond with the purposes of God discovered in Ex 6:2-9 and Amos 4:1-3?

2 God's Reasons for Acting...

God's Reasons for Acting in History to Exalt the Poor and Cast Down the Rich

Main Texts: Luke 1:52-53; Isaiah 3:13-25; Jeremiah 5:26-29; James 5:1-5; Ezekiel 16:46-50

Luke 1:52-53

1   On the basis of the texts cited below, how common a biblical theme is the teaching of Luke 1:53? How many Christians in affluent nations realize how frequently the Bible teaches this? (1 Sam 2:2-8; Job 5:11-16; Ps 10:2-18; 113:5-9; Prov 15:25; Is 1:21-26; 26:5-6; 29:17-21; Ezek 34:11-30; Job 22:5-9; 23:1-2, 12; Job 24:1-12; 19-22; 29:11-17; Ps 37:12-15; 73:2-20; 123:3-4; Prov 20:17; 21:16; Is 10:13-19; Ezek 22:23-31; Hosea 12:7-9; Amos 8:4-8; Micah 6:9-15; Hab 2:5-12; Ezek 22:12).

2   Why does God cast down the rich and exalt the poor?

Isaiah 3:13-25 and Jeremiah 5:26-29

1   Why according to this passage (especially Is 3:14 and Jer 5:26-27) are the ruling classes rich?

2   When and how are they punished? Do you think that God is at work in history in the same way today?

James 5:1-5

1   This text also says the rich became rich by oppression. What application does this teaching (especially v 4) have to the low wages paid to Third World persons who pick our coffee, bananas, etc.

Ezekiel 16:46-50

1   Does this text accuse the rich of the same evil as the texts from Is 3:13-25 and Jer 5:26-29? Is the "sin of oppression" committed by the people of Sodom judged any differently from the active oppression condemned in the previous texts in Isaiah, Jeremiah and James?

3 Siding with the Oppressed

Those Who do Not Side with the Oppressed are Not Really God's People at all

Main Text: Proverbs 14:31; Ecclesiastes 4:1; Isaiah 58:1-10; Matthew 25:31-46

Proverbs 14:31 and Ecclesiastes 4:1

1   Prov 14:31 is typical of a host of texts which command believers to be on the side of the poor. How does Eccles 4:1 help explain why so few people obey this command?
2   Can you see ways in your own life where this happens?

Isaiah 58:1-10

1   How religious do these people seem to be (see v 2)?
2   Is it possible to be involved in oppression of the poor and still worship God? Is it necessary for every person who wants to worship God to be doing the things described in vv 6-7?
3   In light of this passage, how much of the religious activity and worship of people in rich nations is a mockery of the God of the poor?

Matthew 25:31-46

1   Is it an exaggeration to say that this text teaches that church members are not Christians at all (regardless of orthodox theology, charismatic experiences or faithful church attendance) if they do not feed the hungry and side with the poor?
2   Who are the people being judged in v 32? Who are the poor (vv 40, 45)? Does thinking about the persons addressed in the previous parable (Matt 25:14-30) help?
3   Some interpreters think that this passage (and 1 John 3:17) only commands concern for poor Christians. Does Matt 5:43-48 (especially v 44-45) permit or require us to extend the meaning of Matt 25 to all poor everywhere?
4   How would you change your life if you truly believed that aiding the hungry and imprisoned meant ministering to Jesus? And that neglecting the poor meant turning away from God Incarnate lying naked and starving on the roadside?

4 Jubilee Economics

Jubilee Economics and the Redistribution of Wealth

Main Texts: Leviticus 25:8-28

Leviticus 25:8-28

1   Every 50 years, all land is to go back to the original owners — without compensation.

Why did God give this command to his people?

2   What is the theological basis for restoration of land after fifty years? (See v 23).

3   What is the basic "capital" in an agricultural society?

4   Why did God give this regular mechanism rather than merely depend on the charitable inclinations of the rich?

5   Does this passage teach that the right of the original owner to have the means to earn a living is a higher right than the right of the person with enough money to buy the land? (See vv 24-28).

6   Does this passage teach that God is opposed to extremes of wealth and poverty and wills institutionalized mechanisms to avoid that?

7   Is it significant that the year of restoration began on the day of atonement? (See v 9).

8   What would be some appropriate contemporary applications to this Jubilee passage — in the church and in secular society?

9   What would an economic system look like that was designed with this Jubilee passage as a fundamental clue to God's will for the economic realm?

10   Is the basic intent of the legislation on the sabbatical year, tithing, harvesting and interest (for other passages see below) similar to that of Lev 25? (Ex 23:10, 11; Deut 15:1-15; 2 Chron 36:17-21; Neh 10:28-31; Jer 34:8-17; Gen 28:20-22; Lev 27:32; Deut 14:22-29; Deut 26:12-13; Luke 11:42; 23:22; 24:19-22; Ruth 2:19; Ex 22:25-27; Deut 23:19-20; Neh 5:1-12; Ps 15:1-5).

11   If this text teaches that the right to the resources necessary to earn a living is a higher right than the right to private property, what does that say about how the natural resources of nations like the UK should be distributed?

5 Economic Relationships

Economic Relationships in the New Community of Jesus' followers

Main Texts: Acts 2:41-47; 4:32-35; Luke 8:1-3; Mark 10:28-31

Acts 2:41-47; 4:32-35

1   What specific things did Christian fellowship mean for this body of believers?

2   How extensive was their economic sharing?

3   Would it be accurate to say that for the Jerusalem church, Christian fellowship meant unlimited economic liability for and unconditional economic availability to the other sisters and brothers in Christ?

4   Is that what Christian fellowship ought to mean for us today?

5   What was the evangelistic impact of this economic sharing? (See 2:47; 4:33; 6:7).

Luke 8:1-3

1   What instances of economic sharing among Jesus' disciples are there in the Gospels? (See also John 12:16; 13:29).

2   Might the dramatic economic sharing described in Acts 2 and 4 have been an extension of what Jesus had already begun among his disciples?

Mark 10:28-31

1   Was Jesus naive to promise that those who give up everything to follow his will receive 100 times as much in this present age?

2   Is this promise in Mark 10 related to the fact that Jesus' disciples (like the early church) probably engaged in economic sharing so that the resources of one were available to others *as had any need?* If the church were really living that way today, would Jesus' words seem so naive and visionary?

3   How might economic relationships within the body of believers be remodelled along the lines of Lev 25, Acts 2 and Acts 4 today? If they were, would the church be able to present a new model of economic sharing that would be relevant to a world desperately divided between rich and poor?

6 The Pauline Collection

The Pauline Collection: "That There may be Equality" in the World-wide Body of Christ

Main Text: 2 Corinthians 8:1-15

2 Corinthians 8:1-15

1   Why does Paul appeal to the example of Jesus in v 9?

2   What is the guideline for giving presented in vv 13-15? (check several other translations. The RSV has a more literal translation of the Greek: "As a *Matter of equality* your abundance at the present time should supply their want so that (later) their abundance may supply your want, that there may be equality.")

3   How does St. Paul's quotation from Ex 16:18 (in 2 Cor 8:15) help explain his meaning?

4   Is it significant that this Pauline collection (unlike the sharing in the Jerusalem church in one locality) was taken in Europe for Christians in Asia?

5   How far should the Pauline guideline of economic equality be applied today in the world-wide body of Christ?

6   By this offering from Gentile Christians to Jewish Christians, Paul meant to speak a word of reconciliation. How might similar sharing be a reconciling action today?

7   Do you see a consistent pattern in the diverse biblical passages on economic sharing among the people of God such as: Num 26:52-56; Ex 23:10, 11; Deut 15:1-15; 2 Chron 36:17-21; Neh 10:28-31; Jer 34:8-17; Gen 28:20-22; Lev 27:32; Deut 14:22-29; 26: 12, 13; Luke 11:1-2; Lev 19:9, 10; 23:22; Deut 24:19-22; Ruth 2:1-9; Ex 22:25-27; Deut 23:19, 20; Neh 5:1-12; Ps 15:1-5; Matt 5:13-16; 6:1-4; Mk 10:28-31; 35-45; Mk 15:40, 41; Luke 8:1-3; 22:14-20; John 12:6; 13:1-17; 29, 34, 35; Acts 2:41-47; 4:32-37; 6:1-7; 11:27-30; 1 Cor 16:1-4; Acts 21:10-14; 24:10-17; Rom 15:25-29; 2 Cor 8:1-15; 9:1-15; Gal 2:7-10; Rom 12:9-13; 1 Cor 10:16, 17; 11:17-34; 13:1-7; 2 Cor 1:3-7; 11:27-29; Gal 6:9-10; 1 Tim 5:9, 10; Heb 13:1-3; James 2:1-9.

7 Material Abundance

Material Abundance: A Good Gift That can be Dangerous

Main Texts: Ecclesiastes 9:7; Matthew 6:24-33; Matthew 19:16-26

Ecclesiastes 9:7

1   How does this text reflect the biblical attitude towards creation? (See 1 Tim 4:4-5; Gen 1:11-12, 20-22).
2   How biblical is asceticism?

Matthew 6:24-33

1   What is the secret of this carefree attitude towards material possessions?
2   How might the absence of this carefree attitude reflect unbelief? (See vv 26-27, 30). Or an unwillingness to accept Jesus as Lord? (See vv 24, 33).
3   How would the carefree attitude toward possessions advocated by Jesus make us better able to work against hunger and injustice today?

Matthew 19:16-26

1   Why are possessions so dangerous?
2   Do you think that even 1% of the Christians in rich nations actually believe Jesus' statement in vv 23-24?
3   If they did, what would they do?
4   How widespread in scripture is Jesus' attitude toward possessions?
5   Let's assume that most Christians today ought to live a more simple lifestyle. Why? Because simple living is inherently better or because self-denial is necessary while a billion people are malnourished?

8 Obedience and Abundance

Is Material Abundance the Result of Obedience?

Main Texts: Proverbs 6:6-11; Psalm 128:1-4; Psalm 112:1-5, 9; Proverbs 28:27

Proverbs 6:6-11

1   Is poverty sometimes due to laziness?
2   How significant is it that the Bible far more frequently links poverty with oppression than with laziness? (Job 22:5-9; 23:1, 2, 12; 24:1-12, 19-22; 29:11-17; Ps 37:12-15; 73:2-20; 123:3, 4; Prov 20:17; 21:6; 22:16; Is 10:13-19; Ezek 22:23-31; Hosea 12:7-9; Amos 8:4-8; Micah 6:9-15; Hab 2:5-12; James 5:1-6; Ezek 22:12; 2 Thess 3:6, 10, 11, 12;

Prov 11:66; 13:4; 14:23; 20:13; 23:21; 24:30-34; 29:19; 2 Thess 3:11-13).

Psalm 128:1-4

1　Why does God reward obedience with material abundance? Does he always do that?
2　What would the universe be like if virtue regularly was penalized?

Psalm 112:1-5, 9 and Proverbs 28:27

1　How do these texts provide a criterion for knowing whether one's abundance is the result of oppression or obedience which God has rewarded?
2　The obedient person obeys God's commands (Ps 112:1-2). Many biblical passages demonstrate that one of God's most frequent commands is to have concern for the poor, (see Prov 14:21; Ex 22:21-24; 23:9-12; Lev 11:32-34; Deut 24:17, 18; 27:19; Ps 41:12; 72:1-4; 12-14; 82:1-5; Prov 14:31; 21:13; 22:9, 22, 23; 23:10, 11; 29:7; 31:8, 9; Eccles 4:1; Is 32:6-8; 33:14-16; Jer 21:11-12; Luke 11:37-41; 12:32-34; 14:12-14; 19:1-10; Acts 9:36-41; Eph 4:28; James 1:27; Is 1:10-17; 58:1-30; Matt 25:31-46; Luke 3:7-11; 20:45-47; James 2:14-17; 1 John 3:16-18; 4:7, 8; Matt 5:43-48; Deut 10:17-19; Ex 23:1-3; Job 34:18, 19; Rom 1:14-16). Can one then say that those who do not side with the poor can be certain that their material abundance is not the result of God's reward for obedience?
3　Can one give generously to the needy at a time when a billion people are malnourished and still live an affluent lifestyle?

9 God Wills Justice

Main Texts: Psalm 94:1-15; Exodus 23:6-8; Proverbs 13:23; Matthew 5:17-20

Psalm 94:1-15

1　What does this text tell us about the nature of justice?
2　What does this text tell us about the short-term and long-term success of injustice?
3　How does Biblical faith provide the necessary hope for the long, costly struggle for justice?

Exodus 23:6-8 and Proverbs 13:23

1　How do these texts tell us more about what justice is?
2　What contemporary illustrations of Proverbs 13:23 can you think of?

Matthew 5:17-20

1　What does this text say to those who suggest that Jesus had little concern for justice?

10 Systematic Injustice

Sin as Systematic Injustice and Legalized Oppression

Main Texts: Isaiah 5:8-16; 22-24; Isaiah 10:1-4

Isaiah 5:8-16, 22-24

1   Is there any indication that the sin described in v 8 is illegal? Is injustice often legal?
2   What different kinds of sins are condemned in these verses?
3   Are personal sins like alcoholism more or less sinful than participation in structural sins like economic oppression?
4   How does Amos 2:6-8 reflect the same teaching as Is 5:8ff?
5   What structural sin do people in rich nations participate in today?

Isaiah 10:1-4

1   How does this text add to our understanding of structural sin? (See also Ps 94:20ff)
2   Why are unjust laws passed?
3   How similar is this text to the view that laws are merely a reflection of the class interests of the legislators?
4   What does God do to societies that legislate injustice? (See also Ps 94:20ff).

11 Punishment

God's Punishment on Unjust Societies

Main Texts: Micah 3:1-4, 9-12; Jeremiah 22:13-19; Daniel 4:24-28

Micah 3:1-4, 9-12

1   What does the emotion in this passage convey about the depth of God's passion for justice? Should we feel as deeply?
2   What kinds of injustice are condemned here?
3   In what different ways does God intend to punish them? (See vv 4 [cf Amos 8:11-12] and 12 [cf Jer 12:7; Amos 6:7]).
4   What is the attitude of the "religious establishment" to the injustice? (See also Amos 7:10-17). Can you think of modern parables?

Jeremiah 22:13-19

1   What kinds of injustice are condemned here? Do you know of contemporary examples?
2   What does it mean to know God according to this text? (See especially vv 15-16). How should this understanding of the meaning of knowing God correct contemporary

Christian thought?

3   Why does God not always punish unjust rulers as promptly as he did King Jehoiakim?

Daniel 4:24-28

1   Does God deal the same way with non-Jewish rulers as he did with the kings of Israel?

2   Is God at work in history today pulling down unjust rulers and unjust societies?

3   Is UK society sufficiently unjust to deserve the kind of destruction announced by the prophets against Israel and Judah?

12 The Christian's Mandate

Main Texts: Psalm 8:1-9; Matthew 10:37-39; 1 Corinthians 13:1-3

Psalm 8:1-9

1   What is the human mandate for the rest of creation here? (See also Gen 1:26-31).

2   How has this mandate been distorted in the industrialized nations?

3   What is the relationship of persons to God and the rest of creation and how does this relationship condition our mandate?

Matthew 10:37-39

1   Why did Jesus state the cost of discipleship so harshly?

2   What cross will there be today for those who dare to follow in Jesus' steps and implement the biblical teaching on the poor and justice?

3   What cross would you experience this year if you began seriously to implement the biblical teaching on the poor and justice in your life?

4   Can you be Jesus' disciple at all if you fail to do that?

1 Corinthians 13:1-3

1   Persons who become passionately concerned about justice and simple living can easily become harsh and self-righteous. What does this passage tell us about how we should relate to others who have not yet "seen the light"?

The Christian

Four Shorter Studies

1 The Christian in a World of Need

Christian Responsibility to other Christians

1 What does Acts 6:1-6 reveal about:

a   The way the first Christians cared for one another?
b   The kind of people who were chosen to look after the relief programme?

2 Read 2 Corinthians 8:1-24, which deals with a special collection which Paul took from the churches of Asia Minor to the poor in the church at Jerusalem. Then discuss the following questions:

a   What was the attitude to such a fund of Macedonian Christians, whom Paul commended? (vv 1-4).
b   What was the first thing which the Macedonians gave? (v 5). (Does this still apply?)
c   What place should giving for relief have had in the life of the church at Corinth? (v 7).
d   What is the motive which inspires generous Christian giving? (vv 8, 9). See also ch 9 v 5.
e   How does *God* measure the value of our giving? (vv 10-22).
f   How should the principle of equality be worked out in relationships between churches? (13-15).
g   What do those who are in charge of relief funds have to take special care about?

(vv 20, 21). How can they ensure this? (vv 18, 22). What does the phrase 'famous ... for his preaching' (v 18, RSV) suggest about the way such funds were administered?

3 **What does 2 Corinthians 9:1-15 teach us about:**

a   The rewards of giving to help others?

b   The indirect benefits of generosity to needy Christians (vv 11, 12) as they affect the giver?

c   The wider effects of generous giving of this kind? (vv 13, 14). Note the reference to the gospel here.

Christian Responsibility
to the World

1 **Read Matthew 25:31-46. Then discuss the following questions:**

a   Why were the righteous surprised, not knowing what they had really done? Does this suggest anything about our attitude when helping people in need? In this connection look up Matt 6:2. (What is the significance of the word 'When' which Christ used in this verse, when He might have said 'If'?)

b   Consider this statement: 'The righteous were not saved *because* they had fed the hungry and cared for the needy; but doing those things *showed* what they really thought of Christ'. Why does Jesus use the phrase 'prepared for you from the foundation of the world'?

c   What do you understand to be the meaning of v 39 for today?

2 Consider God's comment on the 'consumer' society as spoken through Isaiah (Is 5:8-12) and His call for social justice (Is 10:1-4). What do these mean in *practical* terms to us today?

3 Ezekiel's task was to tell the Jews of his day why it was that God had allowed the Babylonians to capture Jerusalem and carry many of them off into captivity. In chapter 18, Ezekiel challenges their excuses; they said it was all the fault of the older generation (see v 2). Then he tells them what their personal responsibility is – ch 18:5-9. Study these verses. How does all this apply to us today? For instance, is it right to expect interest on money lent to help developing nations? Is the inequality between the Western world and the underdeveloped nations our fault or our predecessors? Does it matter? What can we do about it?

2 The Christian and Material Things

Bible Study Outline Based on Luke 12:13-48

In this study we are concerned with the general question of the Christian's attitude to material things. We shall centre our thinking on a controlling principle laid down by Jesus Himself: "Everyone to whom much is given, of him will much be required" (Luke 12:48). Or as the Living Bible succinctly paraphrases: "To whom much is given much will be required, for their responsibility is greater".

The controlling principle

First, we shall take special care to study the very significant passages which lead up to this saying; they begin at verse 13.

1 There is more to life than material things (vv 13–21)

Read vv 13–21 and ask 'What was wrong with the farmer's decision?' Is it wrong to prosper and to expand a business? The clue is in v 15. Can you define covetousness?

2 Anxiety about food, drink and clothing is a sin (vv 22-31)

Is such anxiety really a *sin*? Why? Sum up Christ's argument here; what truth lies at the heart of it? How would you answer someone who said that this is all right for affluent societies but unrealistic for the under-developed world?

3 The heart of the matter – a matter of the heart (vv 32-34)

"Perfect love casts out fear" (1 John 4:18). How is this truth relevant to this paragraph? 'Life on earth is investment for heaven' – what does this mean in practice?

4 The forgotten factor (vv 35-40)

There is all the difference between living as if we are our own masters, free to do what we want with the world, and living as servants or stewards who will have to answer for our conduct of affairs. Work out what it means at the practical level to be 'ready'.

5 Two ways of waiting (vv 40-47)

Note that *both* kinds of servant expected their master to come back; the bad servant simply thought he would be delayed. Can you sum up the attitude of the bad servant? How does Jesus describe the good one?

6 The key principle (v 48)

All that has gone before is leading up to this. It is therefore to be seen as *the controlling principle* for Christians in their attitudes to material things. Not what is implied in it:

a   We are not the creators, or owners, of material possessions; these are *'given'*: that is, we are stewards who will have to answer for our actions, not owners who can do what they like.

b   The more we have, the more we have to answer for; greater affluence represents greater potential influence, for good or evil.

Reinforcement

We now consider Biblical teaching which reinforces this controlling principle.

1 It was at the heart of the covenant which God made with Israel —

See Deut 8:11-20. If Israel took God's goodness for granted and used it selfishly, she would be judged. Can you find examples of how this worked out in Israel's experience in practice?

2 It was the principle underlying the prophets' condemnation of Israel's behaviour —

See Amos 3:2 — "You only I have known" is a prophetic 'shorthand' for "You are the nation whom I chose and favoured and cared for and provided for ..." Note the significant word 'Therefore ...' See also Hosea 11:1-4 and the vivid picture of Israel as Jehovah's unfaithful wife (ch 2:7, 8) also leading to a 'therefore'. Write a 'therefore' sentence which can be directly applied to Britain.

3 It featured prominently in Christ's teaching

See the parables of the pounds (Luke 19:11-27), the wicked husbandmen (Luke 20:9-18), the talents (Matt 25:14-30). Work out the different emphases given by each of these parables to the controlling principle we are discussing.

4 It was underlined by Paul in his teaching about Christian giving —

2 Cor 9:6-15. Note verse 11 — "enriched ... for ... generosity"; and note how Paul concludes his appeal for giving.

Summary

Does God expect us to follow this principle in a cold and calculating way, or spontaneously and naturally? Consider Matt 25:37, 38, in their setting.

3 The Christian and Developing Countries

A Bible Study to help Christians think through their approach and their attitudes to rural development in Third World countries. It would be helpful to preface the study by reading the booklet: 'Christians and Rural Development' also published by Tear Fund.

Whose World?

Is the earth then the preserve of the strong and a domain for the favoured few? (Job 22:8 NEB)

The Need — Doors Ajar Now

1   At the centre of underdevelopment is injustice. Justice has been defined "that each should receive his due". Is this a Biblical principle? (2 Cor 8:13-14). What do the words of the prophets have to say to us today when we think of the poverty of the Third World? (Amos 6:4, 6; Is 58:6-8).

2   What is God's plan for mankind? (Jer 29:11). What *essential* needs must be met to give welfare and hope?

3   How are Christians to react to physical need? (James 1:27; 2:15-17; 1 John 3:16-18; 1 Tim 2:9-10).

The Opportunity — Meeting Rural People at Their Own Level

1   What needs did Christ meet apart from spiritual ones? (Matt 4:23-24; 11:4-5).

2   How did those who were helped by Jesus and those who watched Him at work feel about Him? (Mark 10:51-52; Luke 7:15-17; John 3:2; John 4:46-53).

3   In what way does practical help add an extra dimension to preaching? (Acts 14:3 and Acts 4:29-30). Is this true in your experience?

4   What incentives do Christians have to get involved in others' poverty? (2 Cor 8:9; Heb 6:10-11).

5   Moses instructed the Israelites on many ways to improve their standards. How comprehensive was this, and why was it really important? (Deut 14:21; 15:10; 20:19-20; 22:1-4; 6-10; 23:12-13, 24-25; 24:19-20; 25:13-15). What response did Moses expect in return? (Deut 28:3-6).

The Organisation — A Tool for Christian Witness through Voluntary Helpers

1   What qualities did the first deacons have that demonstrated their suitability? (Acts 6:3-5,

7-8). How much was a caring ministry shown by other Christians in the Acts?

2 How can village Christians approach others in need and show the authenticity of their Christian faith?

– Through the Missionary or National Leader

3 Study 2 Peter 1:5-8. Try to imagine some of the day by day events and crises in the rural development leader's life from which these qualities might develop.

4 What temperamental quirks might block such personal growth? (2 Cor 12:20; James 3:14-18).

5 What must be absolutely basic to all the planning, thinking and action in a rural development programme? (Prov 3:5-6 and Jer 9:23).

A Part We Can Play

Decide on specific needs arising from this study to pray about either as a group or individually.

Faith in Action

By these actions the integrity of his faith was proved (James 2:22 NEB)

The Methods – Involvement Brings Change

1 Is it right for a Christian to try and raise his standard of living above subsistence level? (Ps 104:14-15; Gen 1:29; 1 Tim 5:8).

2 Prov 30:8-9 might well be the prayer of a subsistence farmer. What attitudes and motives do we have that might prevent us from praying this sincerely?

The Problems – Pitfalls to Recognise

1 If we help to raise living standards, what dangers may follow? (Deut 8:12-14; Luke 12:16-21; 1 Tim 6:8-10).

2 How can these dangers be reduced? (1 Cor 10:31; Deut 8:18).

3 What passages could be used to give warning to these dangers? (i e Haggai 1:2, 6, and 2:18-19). Can you suggest any others?

4 In what ways might a rural development programme be diverted away from meeting people's physical and spiritual needs?

By Bread Alone? — Spiritual Wholeness Includes Facing Civil and Social Responsibilities

1 If Jesus was in the world today how might He reach out to the developing countries? (Mark 9:35-36). What then does He expect from us (Matt 9:37-38 and 10'1). Read Luke 9:12 and 13 and note how the disciples made two suggestions. Both would have limited Christ's impact on the crowd. Do we hinder God's work by the limits of our vision and resources?

2 Even insignificant actions count in Christ's eyes. (Matt 10:42; 25:35-36). He Himself did not despise humdrum service. (John 13:4-5, 12-17). How can Christians today follow this teaching and His example in our own setting? And in the overseas Church?

3 Is practical help a spiritual service? (1 John 2:6; 1 Peter 4:9-11; 1 John 3:17-18; Heb 13:15-16). How can a balance and a wholeness be maintained?

Paul wrote to the Thessalonians: "We remember ... how you put your faith into practice, how your love made you work so hard and how your hope in our Lord Jesus Christ is firm" (TEV 1 Thess 1:3). Elsewhere he talks of the enduring quality of faith, hope and love (1 Cor 13:13). How does each strand play an essential part in the Christian encounter with physical and spiritual need?

4 The Christian Living in a Broken World

The Key is in Jesus

The world we live in is 'broken' by inequality, injustice and rebellion against God. This Bible Study Outline helps us to consider how, as Christians, we should live in the face of this 'brokenness'.

It would be helpful to preface the study by reading the booklet 'Walk in His Shoes' by John Stott, available from Tear Fund.

The example of Jesus

Read Matt 9:35 to 10:15, to see how Jesus lived.

1 How did Jesus set about meeting human need Himself?

2 How does this suggest the need of the world may be met? List the greatest needs today as you see them.

3 How are Christ's followers to set about this task?

The Love of Jesus

Read John 13:31-35 and 1 John 3:14-16. (Note that 'glorified' in John usually refers to the Cross, as it does here).

1 What is the measure of love as Christ defined it?

2 Is it possible for us to love as He loved? How?

3 What happens when such love is demonstrated?

Service, Not Sentiment

Read 1 John 3:17-18 and 2 Cor 6:3-10, and consider what service entails.

1 Answer the question in 1 John 3:17. Do you think this is really so? What are the implications for Christians living in the wealthy West?

2 2 Cor 6:4, 5 lists what others may do to Christians. What does this mean for us today?

3 2 Cor 6:6 lists how Christians respond – can you put these in order of importance? Should we?

Let us look at the teaching of Jesus about serving others. Read Luke 10:25-37 and Matt 25:31-46. What do these passages say about:

1 the people who have a claim on our service?

2 the way we should serve them?

3 the peril of being merely religious?

Consider the ways in which we are equipped to serve. Read 2 Cor 5:20, 21 and John 13:1-15. What do these passages show about:

1 the basic qualifications for serving God?

2 the nature of our task?

LET US REALLY LOVE PEOPLE AND SHOW IT BY OUR ACTIONS 1 John 3:18

How will this Bible Study affect your own life, as a Christian living in a broken world?

Appendix:
Community Health

Community Health

Community Health in the Developing World

Thoughts shared by Dr Diana Forrest (Tear Fund worker in Bangladesh 1975/78)

Background

The kind of work which the average young doctor or nurse does in the West is totally different from the kind of work he will be expected to do if he works on a community health programme in the developing world. His whole approach to the practice of health care needs to change, if he is to be effective in this new situation.

In the West, there has already been developed an advanced and sophisticated health care system. The needs of the seriously ill patients are well cared for in efficiently run hospitals, while there is expert care in the community from G.P.'s, district nurses, health visitors, social workers etc. etc. In the developing world, the health needs of the people are dealt with in a very haphazard fashion, and it would be impossible for them to be able to afford such a sophisticated system as we have in the West.

We who have been trained in the West have not had to think about ways of delivering health care services to our people. This has been worked out already. All we have to do is work efficiently in the system. There has been no need for us to constantly question the system, or if we have questioned it, we have no power ourselves to change it.

The developing world is still trying to work out ways of delivering health care to its people, and is using the help and ideas of expatriates in this. So as we go into health care in a developing country, we cannot go expecting to slot into an already established system, do our work and come home again, leaving the system unchanged. Rather, we need to go expecting to think through the problems for ourselves, and to be actively involved in trying to help the country to develop a health care system which is appropriate for the needs of the people. Such work requires willingness to step out of the security of a well-established hospital system, and to step into the insecurity of working in programmes which are new and experimental. This can either be seen as depressing insecurity or (with God as the driving force behind the ideas) as an exciting challenge.

New Problems

When we enter the developing world, we are immediately faced with new problems which we have not had to deal with before. The four problems which are most commonly faced are:

1 Ignorance
2 Lack of money
3 Malnutrition
4 Poor sanitation and unclean drinking water

1 Ignorance

The ordinary village people are steeped in superstitions and beliefs about ways they should live to keep healthy. It is important to realise this. Ignorance can be thought to mean no knowledge. But in fact their minds are filled with information about health, which is deeply entrenched in tradition. Our first job is to find out what the people believe (*not* to pounce in with lots of teaching!!) Until we have some understanding of their customs and superstitions we shall not be able to teach them in a way which is relevant. Not all their strange practices will need to be condemned. Some may be beneficial, some will not make any difference to health, and some will be harmful. We need to commend the beneficial, ignore those which neither help nor harm, and teach positively against those which are harmful.

2 Lack of Money

In the West (especially in Britain with the NHS) we are not used to asking the question "Can we afford it?" when considering the treatment of a patient. Such a question would be thought to be immoral, since money is no object when dealing with life and death. But the question of money becomes very important when trying to work out a health-care system for the developing world. There is just not enough money to provide sophisticated health care for everybody. Thus we have to make sure that whatever we plan or do is achieved on a limited budget. For example, it would be totally unhelpful to set up a sophisticated outpatient clinic which required imports of thousands of pounds worth of drugs each year. Such a clinic would of course be beneficial to the people it served, but it would set a standard for the country which the Government could not hope to maintain or duplicate, and in the long run it would cause more problems than it solved. Each patient must be treated, not with Western health care standards in mind, but in the context of a country with limited resources. The challenge is to work out ways of preventing and treating disease in as many people as possible as cheaply as possible.

3 Malnutrition

At first sight, the problem of malnutrition appears just to be that of inadequate food. But it does not take long to realise that the problem is far deeper than that. It is one of economics, of education and motivation. It would be all too easy for us to enthusiastically decide that we wanted to help all the malnourished children in the area, and so organise a feeding programme for them. That would, of course, improve the health of a lot of local children. But what would be much more beneficial in the long run (but also much harder work!) would be to teach the mothers how to feed their children *themselves*. The challenge of malnutrition is the challenge of educating and motivating poor people to *produce* and *eat* nutritious foods. This is a long, slow process, and requires a lot of enthusiasm and persistent teaching.

4 Poor Sanitation and Unclean Drinking Water

Latrines and tubewells are not things which doctors and nurses spend much time thinking about in the West, but if we want to improve the health of the people in the developing world, we need to spend a lot of time thinking about them! Again, our ideas need to be appropriate for the country in which we are working. For example, in some areas it may not be possible to organise tubewells for all the people, but they could be encouraged to clean out the ponds from which they drink, and to keep the ponds clean.

Examples of Work...

Some examples of the kind of work which doctors and nurses are involved in when working in community health programmes in the developing world.

The four main areas of work would be:
1 Planning
2 Teaching
3 Clinic work
4 Hospital work

1 Planning

This is something which both doctors and nurses need to be involved in, though more often the responsibility for the planning of the health programme lies on the doctor's shoulders. Plans need to be clearly thought out, written down and worked on to a definite time schedule. They then need to be regularly evaluated and revised. Careful planning, which has been done in consultation with as many people as possible, can save a lot of headaches. Doctors in the developing world, need to be prepared to spend more time thinking and planning and less time in actual medical practice than they are used to.

2 Teaching

The most important role of all doctors and nurses working in a developing country is that of a *teacher*. This cannot be expressed too strongly. If we do not want to teach, we should not go to a developing country. Our main aim should be to teach, and to teach others to teach.

Our natural desire so often is to want to *do* things ourselves, especially in a situation where we know that others cannot do things as well as we can. So often it is much easier to do something ourselves than to try and teach someone else to do it. But if we do not teach, we shall not help the people in the long run. We may build up a very efficient system while we are there, but once we leave, the system will collapse.

While all people should go out with the attitude that they want to teach, some will of course be more involved in teaching than others. The following are some examples of teaching which has to be done: —

The Christian at Work Overseas

a Counterparts

It is common in many development projects for an expatriate to have a national
'counterpart' working alongside him, the idea being for the expatriate to train his counterpart until he is competent to do his job. The expatriate will then leave, and the counterpart
will continue the work.

b All Staff Members

All the national staff working in the project should be receiving health education. This
should include *everybody*, whether they are working directly on the health programme or
not. They should be encouraged to teach all their friends what they have learnt. Often it
is the people who perform the most menial tasks who become the most effective teachers,
because they can communicate with the village people. If we can convince our own staff
to change their ways to improve their health, we have gone a long way towards convincing
many people in the surrounding area.

c Influential People

If the rich, influential people of the area (e g bank managers, pharmacists, businessmen
etc) can be taught and motivated to change their ways to improve their health, they can
greatly influence the poorer people by their example. So even if a health project is mainly
directed towards the poor people, it is still beneficial to spend some time with the rich, if
the teaching is kept as a priority.

d Poor Villagers

It is very important that teaching should reach the level of the poor villagers.
    Some of this teaching can be done in the clinics, but teaching in the actual villages
is important also. It is usually best to teach a national to teach the villagers, since he will
be more on their wave-length.

e Fellow Expatriates

Fellow expatriates should be teaching each other all the time, each willing to draw on the
experience of others, and each willing to share his or her knowledge with the others.

f Formal Training Programmes

The degree of sophistication of a training programme which a worker will be involved in
will depend very much on the country and on the project. Two areas of training which are
becoming popular in developing countries because of their appropriateness are:
    i Medical auxiliary training and
    ii Village health worker training

    i *Medical auxilliaries* are workers who are able to diagnose and treat simple diseases
    in outpatient clinics. They receive much less training than a doctor, but are able to
    deal with at least 80% of the diseases which are presented in an outpatient clinic.

    ii *Village health workers* are village women (who may be illiterate) who teach fellow
    villagers about the prevention of disease, and who treat simple diseases at the village
    level. They are chosen and supported by the people of the village.

When training health workers, our job is to motivate and inspire. The workers will learn a lot from our example (positively or negatively) so we need to be full of inspiration, ideas and enthusiasm.

It is common for the expatriate nurse or doctor to find that he is the first person to do such training in the area, so it is his responsibility to plan the training course and to write the course material.

Teaching well requires a lot of imagination, time and effort. In order to present a complicated subject clearly and simply, one needs to know a lot about it, and to spend time thinking through ways of making the subject-matter interesting and relevant to the people being taught. A useful book on the subject is "Visual Communications Handbook" by Denys Saunders.

Teaching and learning should always be seen as a two-way process. The nationals can help us and teach us a lot. For example, we can learn from them about the local customs and culture, about where we are going wrong in our methods – and they can provide us with a lot of ideas if we are prepared to listen to them. We should not teach pretending we know all the answers; we shall achieve a lot more if we teach the nationals to think up answers to their own problems themselves.

3 Clinic Work

Clinic work may involve setting up new clinics, supervising the running of clinics already established, or sometimes actually diagnosing and treating patients in the clinics. There are two main types of clinics: –

a *General Clinics* where male and female patients of all ages are seen

b *Under Fives Clinics* for children under five years of age, or
   Maternal Child Health Clinics for children under five plus pregnant and nursing mothers. (For detailed and helpful information about Under Five's Clinics see the book "Paediatric Priorities in the Developing World" by David Morley).

In running these clinics the aim should always be for them to be eventually taken over and run by the nationals, so again the priority should be *teaching.*

The emphasis in running the clinics should be on simplicity (i e the costs should be kept low, and the system should be easy for a national to take over). But this does not mean that standards should drop. As much as possible should be done within the limitations of the budget. High standards should be expected and maintained in cleanliness, discipline and in diagnosis in the clinics.

Those treating the patients should see teaching as an important part of treatment, and should be taught to spend time with the patient teaching him about the prevention and treatment of his disease.

4 Hospital Work

In a community health programme, hospital work will take on a low priority, although it is of course important to have a hospital as a referral centre for serious illnesses in the community. A doctor or nurse in a community health programme may well be involved in hospital work. He may be involved in setting up a hospital which will later be taken over by nationals, in supervising some of the hospital workers or in working alongside nationals in a Government-run hospital, teaching them and advising them when necessary.

As in the clinics, so in the hospitals the aim should be to maintain high standards, but to keep to a low budget, and to place a strong emphasis on *teaching*.

Conclusion

Medical work in a developing country is a big challenge! All the time one needs to be inspired with ideas, enthusiasm and persistence. With the Lord as the driving force behind the work, it can be very exciting and fulfilling.

Useful Books for Reading and Reference

Paediatric Priorities in the Developing World — David Morley.
Medical Care in Developing Countries — Maurice King.
Nutrition in Developing Countries — King, Morley and Burgess.
Learning Better Nutrition — Jean A S Ritchie.
Visual Communications Handbook — Denys Saunders.
Child Health Care in Rural Areas — A Manual for Auxiliary Nurse Midwives.
A Medical Laboratory for Developing Countries — Maurice King.

Useful Addresses for Specific Courses and Study Material

British Medical Students Association, BMA House, Tavistock Square, London WC1H 9JP.
Hospital for Tropical Diseases, 5 St Pancras Way, London NW1.
Institute of Child Health, 30 Guildford Street, London WC1N 1EH. (Dr D Morley)
Inter-University Council for Higher Education Overseas, 90-91 Tottenham Court Road, London W1P 0DT.
Liverpool School of Tropical Medicine, Pembroke Place, Liverpool L3 5QA.
London School of Hygiene and Tropical Medicine, Keppel Street, Gower Street, London WC1E 7HT.
Medical Missionary Association, 6 Canonbury Place, London N1 2NJ.
Overseas Development Ministry, Eland House, Stag Place, London SW1E 5DH.
Ross Institute, London School of Hygiene and Tropical Medicine, Keppel Street, Gower Street, London WC1E 7HT.
Missionary School of Medicine, 2 Powis Place, Great Ormond Street, London WC1N 3HT.